Favors
with Flair

Sugared almonds are a traditional wedding favor with a history that stretches back to the ancient Greeks and Romans. Honeyed almonds were considered a delicacy by the Romans and were presented to distinguished guests at important banquets... coating over the slightly bitter almond... is that the wedding couple is ...ether that will include both ...almonds are typically ...embarking on... ...er is indicat...

Favors *with* Flair

75 Easy Designs
for Weddings, Parties, and Events

Mary Lynn Maloney

Creative Publishing
international
Chanhassen, MN

Copyright © 2006
Creative Publishing international, Inc.
18705 Lake Drive East
Chanhassen, Minnesota 55317
1-800-328-3895
www.creativepub.com
All rights reserved

Creative Publishing
international

President/CEO: Ken Fund
Vice President/Publisher: Linda Ball
Vice President/Retail Sales: Kevin Haas

Executive Editor: Alison Brown Cerier
Senior Editor: Linda Neubauer
Creative Director: Brad Springer
Cover & Book Design: Lois Stanfield
Photo Stylist: Joanne Wawra
Photo Art Director: Tim Himsel
Photographer: Andrea Rugg

Library of Congress Cataloging-in-Publication Data

Maloney, Mary Lynn.
  Favors with flair : 75 easy designs for weddings, parties,
and events
/ by Mary Lynn Maloney.
     p. cm.
  ISBN 1-58923-208-9 (soft cover)
  1. Party decorations. 2. Wedding decorations. 3. Holiday
decorations. 4. Handicraft. I. Title.
  TT900.P3.M35 2005
  745.594'1--dc22

                              2005010048

Printed in U.S.A.
10 9 8 7 6 5 4 3

In loving memory
of my sister,
Eileen Maloney Szydlo
1963–2003

About the Author

Mary Lynn Maloney is a mixed-media artist, designer, and teacher whose projects and articles are regularly featured in crafting magazines and books. She has a background in graphic design, a degree in arts and humanities, and a passion for creativity. Her love of history, literature, art, and travel often influence her finished designs, giving her work a sense of another place or time. Mary Lynn likes to look at common art materials with a slightly different perspective and delights in creating things that are a bit unconventional or unexpected.

Acknowledgments

A very special thank you to my parents, Jim and Shirley Maloney. Their encouragement of imagination, reading, and resourcefulness provided an ideal environment in which creativity thrived. Thanks to my former graphic design professor and long-time friend, Judi Kauffman, for her big heart and savvy advice. Sincere thanks to the many manufacturers who supplied products for this book. Thanks to Alison Brown Cerier for being an ideal editor and giving me lots of creative elbow room. Many thanks to editor Linda Neubauer for her helpful comments and precise eye. Thanks to my culinary idols, Ben and Judy Stewart, for their recipe ideas and inspiration. And finally, a big bunch of love and thanks to my husband, Victor Judd, for his confidence, perspective, and ready laughter.

Contents

6   Crafting Favors

11 For a Romantic Wedding

13   Candied Almonds Cone
14   Savor Love Candy Roll
15   Love Letter Stamps
16   Message Hearts
17   Spirals Candy Tin
18   Iridescent Hearts Box
19   Sheer Bag with Bells
21   Translucent Heart
22   Festive Mini Champagne Glass
23   Scrollwork Potpourri Box
24   Heart Magnet Tin
25   Bee Mine Honey Jar
27   Jump the Broom
28   Charmed Slide Frame
29   Art Paper Packet
30   Sweethearts Cookie Cutter
31   Pearl-Wrapped CD Envelope
33   Custom Blend Tea Package
34   Fore! Ever
35   Message in a Bottle
36   Modern Tussie-Mussie
37   Love Sonnet Journal Cover
38   Glittering Basket

39 For Women

41 Mini Shopping Tote
42 Ribboned Bag
43 Funky Fibers Trinket Box
44 Flower-Topped Box
45 Treasured Friends Stickpin
47 Soy Candles on the Half Shell
48 Bling Keeper
49 Etched Mirror in Suede Pouch
51 Antiqued Mini Frame
52 Alphabet Eyeglass Case
53 Grosgrain Ribbon Bookmark
55 Bath Fizzy Bonbons
56 Molded Glycerin Soap
57 Custom Bath Salts
58 Keepsake Photo Album

59 Just for Fun

61 Japanese Basket
62 Sun and Fun Rubber Ducky
63 Plumed Pen
65 Movie Night Popcorn Box
66 Wine Stopper with Knob Top
67 Wine-Tasting Journal
69 Card Party Coaster
70 New Address Tag
71 BBQ Spice Rub Crate
72 BBQ Badge and Bandana
74 Stamped Chinese Door Hanger
75 Irish Charm Pin
76 Glow Stick Necklace

77 For Life Celebrations

79 Pink or Blue Coin Towers
80 Cherubic Dusting Powder
81 Stenciled Baby Buggy Box
82 Handkerchief Bundle of Joy
84 Precious Baby Votive
85 Quinceañera Ribbon
86 Decorative Cross River Rocks
87 Celtic Cross Bookmark
88 Graduation Party Pocket
89 Smartie Lightbulb
91 Silver Anniversary Photo Holder
92 Fabulous Fifty Golden Pushpins

93 For Holiday Parties

95 Ring in the New Year!
96 Key to My Heart
97 Spring Flowers to Go
98 Patriotic Sparklers
99 Halloween Treat Bag
100 Thanksgiving Pyramid
101 Hanukkah Candle Set
103 Mitten Clip Place Card
104 Jingle Bell Bucket
105 Joy Candle Wrap
107 Jar of Christmas Mocha
108 Frankincense Pouch

109 Patterns

111 Sources

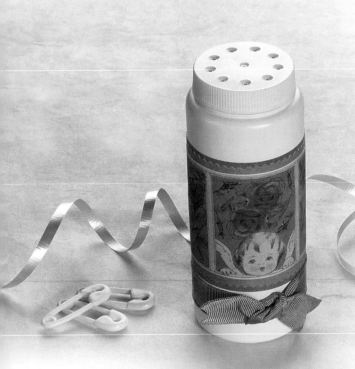

Crafting Favors

Favors are a charming aspect of hospitality—a small token of thanks and regard for your guests. Favors also serve as keepsakes, reminding recipients of their time spent at your event. This gracious tradition has become an essential element of weddings and all sorts of parties, celebrations, and events.

Because favors are so easily customized, they're an ideal way to add a personal touch to your festivities. That's why they are popular do-it-yourself projects, even among people who wouldn't call themselves crafters. Favors need not be extravagant or costly either. A little inspiration and a handful of craft materials are all you need.

Favors with Flair presents seventy-five favors ranging from elegant to whimsical, thoughtful to playful. Each is an original design, so your favors will stand out from the ordinary. These clever projects are for weddings of many styles, gatherings of women (bridal showers, birthdays, book clubs, and so on), fun parties (barbecues, wine tastings, pool parties), life celebrations (baby showers, graduations, milestone birthdays), and holiday parties throughout the year. While the favors are divided into categories, look through the whole collection. You may find the perfect favor for your event in an unexpected place. For example, the BBQ Badge and Bandana would be great for a wedding with a Texas theme. Many favors can be easily adapted for different events, too.

First, Relax!

All the projects are easy to assemble. You'll be making multiples—maybe even hundreds!—so that's important. For each favor, there is a detailed list of the supplies and tools you will need. If you want to know the exact product, check the sources list at the back of the book. Otherwise, you will find many similar options while you are shopping.

Some of the projects are very quick, and others take a bit more time. There are tips on how to scale back some of the more involved projects if you are short on time. A popular strategy is to gather some friends to help with the favors. Brides, gather your attendants, and set up an assembly line to make your favors a few weeks before the wedding. There's sure to be lots of laughter, and it's a nice way for bridesmaids to get together in a casual setting.

These favors are lots of fun to make, so relax and enjoy the creative process. Although you should take care that your favors are neatly made, they do not have to be cookie-cutter perfect. In fact, you don't *want* them to look as though they were just bought in a store. The charm of a hand-crafted item lies in the slight imperfections that reveal the human touch and the love that went into its creation.

Buying Supplies

Materials for favors can be found almost anywhere you shop. Craft and fabric stores, rubber stamp and scrapbook shops, discount and import stores, specialty ribbon and yarn shops, hardware and office supply stores, and online shops were all sources for the projects in this book. Keep your eyes (and your mind) open as you look around for materials. Take time to stroll through a shop and look at things with a creative eye. Wander down a craft store aisle you might not normally visit. A miniature teapot you find in the dollhouse aisle, for example, might strike you as the perfect embellishment for a bridal shower favor. There are plenty of pretty wedding favor containers on the market that are perfect starting points; all they need is your own personal touch to take them from nice to knockout.

Many favors can be enhanced with clip art images that are copied and printed on your home computer. Clip art is available both in book and electronic formats. Dover Publications offers an extensive line of clip art images for nearly every subject imaginable. The Vintage Workshop is a reliable source for beautiful vintage images in downloadable and CD format.

I make it a practice to "share the wealth" with a variety of businesses when shopping for craft materials. Large stores offer an attractive mix of convenience and wide selection. Local, independent shops are eager to share their considerable product knowledge and can offer exceptional customer service. With so many specialized Web sites out there, online ordering is very popular, and it's especially handy for people who don't live near large urban shopping areas. Online suppliers are probably your best bet for getting a special rate when buying supplies in bulk. A thorough Internet search for wedding or party favors or for a specific product should yield plenty of sources to get you started in the right direction. This could be an important consideration if you need to make 250 favors! The source list on page 111 will help you find some of the special items used for the favors.

Common Scents

When using candles, sachets, or potpourri in your favors, consider that some guests may be sensitive or even allergic to certain fragrances. Although jasmine smells like heaven to you, it could give Aunt Lois a splitting headache. Wrap any scented favors in pretty paper, glassine, or fabric envelopes. Contain large amounts of potpourri inside a closed box. Also, if you choose to incorporate candles into your favors or centerpieces, don't use scented candles on tables where food will be served. You don't want a candle scent competing with the aroma of your main course.

Making Multiples

The materials list and instructions for each project are written for one favor. Obviously you will need to multiply the amounts by the number of favors you want to make. Whether you need to make 10 favors or 200, there are ways to save time, make the most of your supplies, and help the production process move smoothly. It is usually more time-efficient to complete each step for all the favors before moving to the next step. This allows drying time for glues, inks, or paints between steps. Ribbons and paper shapes can be cut all at once, so you don't repeatedly pick up and put down scissors.

For favors that include a personalized message, the directions tell you how to create multiples efficiently, using your computer and printer. A word processing or page layout program gives you lots of font and formatting options so you can achieve just the typestyle and size you want. Once your message is typed, your program allows you to quickly "gang," or copy and paste, your message so it fills the page. You can then print your document in black or colored ink onto the printer-compatible paper of your choice. You can save a great deal of time at this stage by applying an adhesive to the entire back of your printed page *before* you cut out the individual messages. Spray the back of the paper with an aerosol adhesive, or roll it through an adhesive application system (Xyron®), which essentially turns your paper into a sticker. Then each message can be cut out and quickly adhered to a tag which is attached to the favor.

When the directions tell you to cut out printed text in a circle, use a hole punch of the correct diameter to speed up the process. Hole punches are available in many sizes. Simply turn the punch over and feed the paper in with the printed side toward you so you can center the text in the hole.

Whenever you need to cut multiple lengths of ribbon, take steps to prevent fraying before you cut. Measure the ribbons and mark where you intend to cut them. Then apply a liquid fray preventer, such as Fray Check™, across the ribbons at all the marks. Allow them to dry and then cut the ribbons.

The directions for several favors include hand-tearing of paper. Once your message is typeset and printed, simply hold the page in your hands and tear slowly around the printed text. Deckle-blade scissors can also be used to cut pieces quickly and still give the edges a torn look. Deckle-edge rulers are also available and can help save time when a torn look is desired on a straight edge. Simply lay the ruler down on the paper, hold it steady with one hand, and tear the paper up toward you with the other hand.

Presenting Your Favors

There are many ways to present favors to your guests. Favors can coordinate with the table decorations and be placed at each place setting. They might be gathered on a tray and become a table centerpiece. Favors can be creatively grouped on a sideboard or table and accompanied by an attractive sign that invites guests to help themselves to a tiny token. Or consider asking a young, responsible friend or relative to pass out favors; she or he would probably be excited and honored to help.

for a Romantic Wedding

Sugared almonds are a traditional wedding favor with a history that stretches back to the ancient Greeks and Romans. Honeyed almonds were considered a delicacy by the Romans and were presented to distinguished guests at important banquets and [illegible] coating over the slightly bitter almonds that the wedding couple is [illegible]ember [illegible] ether that will include both [illegible] lmonds are typically [illegible]er is m[illegible]

Candied Almonds Cone

A pretty note explaining the history behind giving sugared almonds at weddings adds interest and meaning to this centuries-old tradition.

You will need

- Cone template (page 109)
- Tracing paper
- Pencil
- Gold crinkle texture paper
- Scissors
- Glue stick
- Peacock feather strands
- Fabric glue
- Computer and printer
- Light ivory floral printed cardstock, 8½" × 11" (21.8 × 28 cm)
- Text panel template (page 109)
- Sugared almonds, five per cone

TRADITION TEXT

Sugared almonds are a traditional wedding favor with a history that stretches back to the ancient Greeks and Romans. Honeyed almonds were considered a delicacy by the Romans and were presented to distinguished guests at important banquets. The candy coating over the slightly bitter almond illustrates that the wedding couple is embarking on a life together that will include both the bitter and the sweet. Five almonds are typically given to each guest. An odd number is indivisible and suggests that, from hereafter, the couple is as well. The five almonds represent five distinct wishes for the bride and groom: health, wealth, happiness, fertility, and longevity.

1 With a pencil, trace the cone template onto tracing paper and cut it out. Trace around the template on a sheet of the gold paper and cut it out. Roll it into a cone shape and glue it in place. Knot together a small bundle of peacock feather strands, using one of the strands. Glue the bundle to the front seam of the cone with a dab of fabric glue.

2 Create a 3" × 3¾" (7.5 × 9.5 cm) text box in a word processing document on the computer. Type in the sugared almond tradition text (at left), using the desired font in a size to fit the box. Copy the box three times and center one box in each quadrant of the page. Print it on the ivory cardstock.

3 Trace the text panel template onto tracing paper; cut it out. Center the template over the printed text and trace around it. Cut out the text panel. Insert the text panel into the cone and add five sugared almonds

TIP To save time, print the text panels on 3½" (9 cm) squares and simply cut them apart, eliminating the scalloped edge in step 3.

Savor Love Candy Roll

These dressed-up Life*savers* playfully remind wedding guests to *savor* the love in their lives.

You will need

- Roll of Lifesavers® candies
- Earth-toned striped paper
- Ruler
- Pencil
- Scissors
- Glue stick
- Self-adhesive pastel alphabet stickers, ¼" (6 mm) high
- Compass
- Light blue cardstock
- Yellow cardstock
- ⅛" (3 mm) hole punch
- Computer and printer
- Yellow paper ¼" (6 mm) hole punch
- 8" (20.5 cm) blue yarn
- 1½" (3.8 cm) and 1" (2.5 cm) hole punches, optional

1 Carefully remove the outer wrapper from the roll of candy. Cut the striped paper to the size of the outer wrapper. Roll the candy in the striped paper and secure with dabs of glue

2 Cut a piece of the striped paper to a 2⅜" × ½" (6.2 × 1.3 cm) strip. Spell out "savor love" with the alphabet stickers onto the strip of paper. Glue the strip onto the candy roll.

3 Draw a 1½" (3.8 cm) circle on the blue cardstock, using a compass. Cut out the circle and glue it onto the yellow cardstock. Cut the yellow cardstock even with the edge of the blue circle. Punch a ⅛" (3 mm) hole near the edge of the circle.

4 Create a 1" (2.5 cm) text circle in a word processing document on the computer. Type the wedding couple's name and date in the circle, leaving the center ¼" (6 mm) of the circle blank. Copy the circle as many times as will fit on the page. Print it on the yellow paper. Cut out a circle and glue it to the center of the blue side of the tag. Punch a ¼" (6 mm) circle from blue cardstock and glue it onto the center of the yellow paper circle.

5 Tie the blue yarn around the right edge of the candy roll. Tie the other end of the yarn through the hole in the tag and knot to secure. Trim any excess yarn.

TIP **Instead of spelling out "savor love" with the alphabet stickers, include the message in the typed text box as part of the tag. This will save a little time and money. Also, instead of using a compass to draw the circles, you can buy 1½" (3.8 cm) and 1" (2.5 cm) hole punches to cut the circles quickly.**

Love Letter Stamps

Postage stamps are an affordable way to add art and color to a favor. This petite packet is both pretty and practical: a romantic stamp adorns the cover, and two more stamps are tucked inside for your guest's love letters.

You will need

- Pastel striped paper
- Scissors
- Gold coin envelope
- Glue stick
- Narrow orange satin ribbon
- Three "I Love You" postage stamps
- Green cardstock
- Orange cardstock
- Computer and printer
- Pink paper

1 Cut the pastel striped paper to a 1" (2.5 cm) wide band. Wrap the band around the coin envelope and glue the ends of the band together on the back of the envelope, trimming any excess paper. Wrap the narrow orange ribbon around the paper band and glue the ends together on the back.

2 Stick one stamp to the green cardstock. Trim the cardstock closely around the stamp, leaving a narrow border. Adhere this trimmed piece onto the orange cardstock. Trim, leaving a narrow border. Glue the assembled postage stamp to the front of the envelope, over the center of the band.

3 Create a 1¾" × 2½" (4.5 × 6.5 cm) text box in a word processing document on the computer. Type the John Donne quote ". . . letters mingle souls" and the wedding couple's names in the box. Copy the box as many times as will fit on the page. Print it on the pink paper and cut out a square note. Cut two postage stamps from their sheet, leaving the protective paper backing in place. Insert the printed quote and the stamps into the envelope.

TIP **Change the stamp and message to suit your occasion. A floral stamp, for example, could be used for a garden club fundraiser lunch or a Mother's Day tea with the simple message "Spring has sprung!" Stamps showcasing vintage toys might be just right for an anniversary party. A stamp commemorating a particular profession is ideal for a retirement party.**

Message Hearts

This is a very quick and easy way to give a plain box some cool style. This favor is also appropriate for a Valentine's Day event.

You will need

- 2" × 2" × 1¼ " (5 × 5 × 3.2 cm) clear acrylic box
- 8" (20.5 cm) of pink/multi striped grosgrain ribbon, 1½ " (39 mm) wide
- Scissors
- Fabric glue
- "Follow your heart" woven tag

1 Glue the striped ribbon horizontally around the entire box. Trim any excess ribbon.

2 Glue the woven tag on top of the ribbon on the center front of the box.

3 Fill the box with candy message hearts.

TIP Woven tags, available in scrapbooking stores, come in a variety of sentiments. Choose a tag to suit the occasion and fill the box with related sweets. For example, a tag that celebrates Easter or spring works well with robin's egg candies. "It's a Boy" or "It's a Girl" tags can be used along with blue or pink jelly beans for a baby shower.

Spirals Candy Tin

The spiral is a symbol of continuity or eternity in many cultures, making it an especially meaningful element of a wedding favor. These modern spirals are colorful and fun, too.

You will need

- 2" (5 cm) metal tin with glass lid
- Dimensional adhesive, such as Diamond Glaze™
- Spiral stickers, assorted bright colors
- Toothpick
- Narrow yellow satin ribbon
- Fabric glue
- Scissors
- ¾" (2 cm) circle punch
- Orange cardstock
- Green "forever" label sticker
- Sugared almonds or other candy

1 Cover the inside area of the glass lid with a thin, even layer of the dimensional adhesive. Press the spiral stickers into the adhesive, right sides down, using the toothpick. Allow the glaze to dry completely.

2 Glue the yellow ribbon around the outer edge of the lid, using fabric glue. Tie the ribbon into a knot and trim any excess.

3 Punch a circle from the orange cardstock. Center the circle on top of the lid. Apply the "forever" sticker across the orange circle, securing the circle and sticker to the lid.

4 Fill the tin with candy; sugared almonds are traditional for a wedding.

Iridescent Hearts Box

Y ou may recognize this acrylic box; it's a common wedding favor and is sold in the wedding crafts department. A bit of embellishment changes it from nice to nifty.

You will need

- Joined hearts acrylic favor box
- Sapphire blue alcohol-based ink
- 10 " (25.5 cm) each of three decorative fibers: purple, green, metallic
- Tacky glue
- "Adore" self-adhesive glossy dimensional sticker
- Scissors

1 Remove the lid from the acrylic box. Squeeze the sapphire ink directly from the bottle into the inside of the box lid. Cover the lid evenly and completely. Allow the ink to dry.

2 Knot the decorative fibers together at one end. Glue the knot to the top of the box lid. Arrange the loose ends of the fibers in a graceful curve across the box top. Adhere the "adore" sticker over the fibers and onto the box top. Trim the fibers, allowing some to dangle off the left side of the box top.

Sheer Bag with Bells

T his is a festive but simple way to give traditional sugared almonds at a winter wedding.

You will need

- Purple organza drawstring favor bag
- Five sugared almonds
- Large silver jingle bell
- Two small silver jingle bells

1 Fill the organza bag with the sugared almonds, and close the bag with the ribbon drawstrings.

2 Thread the large jingle bell onto one ribbon and push the bell up against the gathered neck of the bag. Tie the drawstrings into a bow.

3 Thread the smaller jingle bells onto the ribbon tails and knot the ribbon ends to secure the bells.

TIP These are great all-purpose bags that are inexpensive, elegant, and a snap to customize for a particular theme or event. For a springtime wedding or an Easter gathering, glue small silk flowers to the ends of the drawstrings. For a baby shower, thread black-and-white letter beads to spell out "boy" or "girl" along the ribbon ends. For an anniversary party, use large, inexpensive vintage-looking buttons as a focal point and pull the drawstring ribbons through the buttonholes or shanks.

Thank you for sharing our day.
Mark & Laura
June 12

Translucent Heart

This subtly swirled glass heart is ideal for a wedding that takes place during the holidays. Your guests will remember your special event every year when it's time to trim the tree.

You will need

- Glass heart ornament
- Transparent glass paints in orange, white, and burgundy
- Parchment baking paper
- Computer and printer
- White cardstock
- Ruler
- Scissors
- ⅛" (3 mm) hole punch
- 12" (30.5 cm) each of pink and orange textured fibers

1 Remove the hanger cap from the glass ornament. Squeeze the orange paint randomly inside the ornament. Follow with the white paint, then the burgundy, swirling the paint by moving the ornament around. Turn the ornament upside down on a large sheet of parchment paper, allowing the paints to run out of the ornament and puddle on the parchment. Allow the paints to dry thoroughly. Replace the hanger cap.

2 Create a 2¼" × ¾" (6 × 2 cm) text box in a word processing document on the computer. Type in your personal message. Copy the box as many times as will fit on the page, leaving a small margin around each box. Print it on the white cardstock.

3 Cut the messages into 2½" × 1" (6.5 × 2.5 cm) rectangles. Punch the lower left corner with a hole punch. Thread the orange and pink fibers through the tag and tie them onto the ornament hanger wire.

TIP Transparent paints look opaque when wet but dry to a transparent finish. The painting process itself is very free-form. No two ornaments will look exactly alike. Drying time can take as long as 24 hours, so plan accordingly.

Festive Mini Champagne Glass

You can easily jazz up the common favor of a miniature champagne glass with a little wire and beads. Leave the glass empty, or fill it with small candies or a tea light candle.

You will need

- Mini champagne glass favor
- 20" (51 cm) hot pink craft wire, 22-gauge
- Flat-nose jewelry pliers
- 16 to 18 assorted glass beads
- Pencil

1 Wrap the wire randomly around the stem of the champagne glass, beginning at the base. Here and there, string a few beads onto the wire as you wrap. Secure the beads by twisting the wire, then coiling it a few times around the tip of a pencil.

2 Bend the end of the wire into the bowl of the glass and pinch down to secure.

TIP **Champagne glass favors are also appropriate for milestone birthdays, fundraisers, and New Year's celebrations.**

Scrollwork Potpourri Box

The openwork design on this box top makes it an ideal container for potpourri. Use the color combination shown here or personalize the box with craft paint and ribbon in your wedding colors.

You will need

- Round papier-mâché box with wire scrollwork lid
- Sage green paint
- Paintbrush
- Rust satin ribbon, 1½" (39 mm) wide
- Scissors
- Fabric glue
- "Love" self-adhesive dimensional sticker
- Tacky glue
- Permanent marker
- Small manila shipping tag
- 6" (15 cm) sage green grosgrain ribbon, ¼" (7 mm) wide
- Small cellophane bag
- Potpourri

1 Paint the bottom and lower third of the box with the sage green paint. Allow the paint to dry. Glue the rust ribbon around the box, leaving a small area of the green paint showing at the bottom.

2 Remove the paper backing from the sticker. Adhere the sticker to the center of the box lid using the tacky glue for extra hold.

3 Write a personal message on the manila tag. Loop the sage green ribbon through the tag. Tie the ribbon to the side of the scrollwork box lid.

4 Fill the small cellophane bag with potpourri and close the top. Insert the bag into the box and cover it with the lid.

TIP Instead of potpourri, fill the box with bath oil beads, crocus bulbs, or wrapped candies. With a different sticker, this favor is also suitable for bridal showers, garden club meetings, and other events.

Heart Magnet Tin

T his tiny tin holds a little magnet that is not only elegant, but useful.

You will need

- Sage green mulberry paper
- 2½" × 2" (6.5 × 5 cm) hinged stainless steel box
- Matte acrylic adhesive
- Water and mixing cup
- Paintbrush
- Decorative scrollwork print paper
- Scissors
- Computer and printer
- White speckled paper
- Celadon green pigment inkpad
- Glue stick
- Mat board
- Craft knife and cutting mat
- Peacock blue ribbon
- Fabric glue
- Two magnet strips, ½" × 1" (1.3 × 2.5 cm)
- Heart-shaped wood cutout

1 Tear the mulberry paper to the shape of the box lid. Mix the acrylic adhesive with a little water. Brush the lid with a thin layer of the mixture and press the paper in place. Brush another layer of diluted adhesive over the paper. Allow to dry. Cut a ½" × 2¾" (1.3 × 7 cm) strip of the scrollwork paper and adhere it the same way to the lid. Allow to dry.

2 Create a ¾" × 2¼" (2 × 6 cm) text box in a word processing document on the computer.

Center the wedding couple's name and date in the box. Copy the box as many times as will fit on the page. Create a ⅝" × 3" (1.5 × 7.5 cm) text box in another document. Type the definition of magnetize in the box. Copy the box as many times as will fit on the page. Print both on the white paper.

3 Cut out the couple's names and wedding date. Apply the celadon ink directly from the inkpad to the edges of the paper. When dry, glue the text to the box lid, using the glue stick.

4 Cut out the definition of magnetize. Adhere the definition to the inside bottom of the box, using the glue stick.

5 Cut a rectangle of mat board 1¼" × 1" (3.2 × 2.5 cm), using a craft knife and cutting mat. Cover the rectangle with the peacock blue ribbon, using the fabric glue. Wrap the ribbon around to the back of the mat board and neatly glue down all the edges. Use a generous amount of fabric glue to adhere the magnet strips to the back of the mat board.

6 Brush the wooden heart with the diluted glue. Cover the heart with the print paper, folding the paper around to the back of the heart. Brush the covered heart with another layer of diluted glue. Allow it to dry. Adhere the heart to the center of the ribbon-covered mat board, using the fabric glue. Place the magnet inside the box lid.

Bee Mine Honey Jar

Honey is a natural sweetener and is a charming reminder of the pure and simple quality of love. Small jars of honey are available from Be My Honey (see sources, page 111).

You will need

- 4-oz jar of honey
- Ruler
- Scissors
- Blue and white swirl print paper
- Craft glue
- 4" (10 cm) narrow mauve satin ribbon
- Green and white swirl print paper
- 1⅛" (2.8 cm) circle punch
- Round white tag with metal rim, 1¼" (3.2 cm) in diameter
- Computer and printer
- White paper
- Glue stick

1 Cut the blue swirl paper into a ½" × 4 ½" (1.3 × 11.5 cm) strip. Adhere the strip across the top and down the sides of the honey jar, using craft glue. Glue the mauve ribbon to the center of the blue strip.

2 Punch two circles from the green swirl paper. Glue one circle to the center of the white tag.

3 Create a ⅞" (2.2 cm) text circle in a word processing document on the computer. Type the wedding couple's names inside the circle. Copy the circle as many times as will fit on the page, leaving a margin around each circle. Print it on the white paper. Cut out the text circle and glue it onto the tag, using the glue stick. Lay the strings of the tag across the lid of the honey jar. Glue the remaining green circle over the strings, attaching the tag to the jar lid.

4 Create a ¾" (2 cm) text circle in a word processing document on the computer. Type "Bee Mine" inside the circle. Copy the circle as many times as will fit on the page, leaving a margin around each circle. Print the text on the white paper. Cut out the text circle and glue it to the center top of the jar lid, using the glue stick.

"Jumping The Broom" represents a leap taken by the bride and groom into the new realm of married life. It is a tradition that originated long ago in West Africa, and was practiced during slavery as a way to honor a couple's cultural heritage. The tradition continues today as a celebration of a rich legacy, and a symbol of commitment.

Jump the Broom

Many African-American couples choose to incorporate "jumping the broom" into their wedding service. This keepsake comes with a tag explaining the tradition. Look for these tiny brooms in the floral areas of craft stores.

You will need

- 6" (15 cm) maroon trim
- Mini straw broom
- Fabric glue
- Scissors
- ½ yd. (0.5 m) multicolor decorative fiber
- Dark sage pigment inkpad
- 1½ " × 3" (3.8 × 7.5 cm) manila tag
- Computer and printer
- Light orange paper, 8 ½ " × 11" (21.8 × 28 cm)
- Glue stick

Tag Text

"Jumping the Broom" represents a leap taken by the bride and groom into the new realm of married life. It is a tradition that originated long ago in West Africa and was practiced during slavery as a way to honor a couple's cultural heritage. The tradition continues today as a celebration of a rich legacy and a symbol of commitment.

1 Cut the maroon trim in half. Wrap and glue the trim around the top and base of the broom handle; trim any excess. Cut two lengths of the multicolor fiber to 6" (15 cm). Knot the strands around the base of the broom handle.

2 Tap the dark sage inkpad along the edges of the manila tag, creating a thin border around the tag. Allow the ink to dry.

3 Create a 2⅜" × 1¼" (6.2 × 3.2 cm) text box in a word processing document on the computer. Type in the tag text (at left), using the desired font in a size to fit the box. Copy the box as many times as will fit on the page. Print it on the orange paper.

4 Cut out the text and glue it onto the manila tag. Tie the tag to the broom with the remaining multicolored fiber.

We thank you
for sharing
our special day!

Much Love,
Laura & Mark

Charmed Slide Frame

A slide mount frame can become a miniature photo frame. Currently a hot item for scrapbooking, slide mount frames are available in craft, rubber stamping, and scrapbooking stores. This is a perfect favor for a couple with a sense of fun and creativity.

You will need

- Black cardstock
- Scissors
- Brown cardstock slide mount frame
- Photograph of wedding couple to fit a
  1" × 1½" (2.5 × 3.8 cm) opening
- Glue stick
- Computer and printer
- White paper
- Alphabet stickers
- Copper page tab charm
- Silver heart charm
- Jewelry pliers

1 Cut two pieces of black cardstock to fit the inside panels of the slide mount. Round the corners as necessary. Cut the photograph slightly larger than the open area of the slide mount and glue it to the back of one black cardstock piece.

(Check to be sure the photo will be centered in the opening.) Glue the mounted photo to the inside front panel.

2 Glue the other piece of the black cardstock over the inside back panel of the slide mount. Create a 1½" × 2" (3.8 × 5 cm) text box in a word processing document on the computer. Type a message and the wedding couple's names in white text reversing out of a black background. Copy the box as many times as will fit on the page. Print it on the white paper. Cut out the message and glue it onto the inside back panel of the slide mount.

3 Spell out the word "joy" with the letter stickers on the oval area of the page tab charm. Use the jewelry pliers to open the jump ring of the heart charm and attach the charm to the ring of the page tab. Slide the page tab diagonally onto the top right corner of the slide mount.

Art Paper Packet

I t's easy to customize the template used in this project to the size and proportion you want. Fill the envelope with a chocolate coin, a favorite poem, a photograph, or a lottery ticket.

You will need

- Tea bag envelope template (page 110), taken from Fit-It CD by Red Castle (see sources page 112)
- Pencil
- White paper
- Scissors
- Handmade paper with leaf inclusions
- Glue stick
- 10" (25.5 cm) black/ivory striped ribbon, ⅜" (9 mm) wide
- Heart-shaped copper ribbon buckle
- Computer and printer
- Colored paper

1 Trace the tea bag template onto the white paper. Cut it out.

2 Lay the handmade paper right-side down on your work surface. Place the template over the paper and trace around it. Lightly mark the fold lines shown on the template. Carefully cut the shape from the handmade paper.

3 Fold the envelope along the dotted lines that were transferred from the template. Glue the sides of envelope closed.

4 Insert the striped ribbon through the copper heart ribbon buckle. Slide the buckle to the center of the ribbon. Glue the striped ribbon horizontally around the envelope just below the opening, placing the heart buckle in the center. Trim any excess ribbon.

5 Create a 1¾" (4.5 cm) text circle on the computer. Type the couple's names in the circle. Copy the circle as many times as will fit on the page. Print it on the colored paper. Trim the circle and glue to the flap of the tea bag envelope. Tuck the flap into the envelope slot.

TIP **This favor is so versatile because of all the wonderful papers on the market today. The right paper and small embellishment can tailor the packet for any occasion.**

Sweethearts Cookie Cutter

A heart-shaped cookie cutter is the beginning of this sentimental, nostalgic favor. The cutter is not only part of the favor, but also the template for cutting out the paper heart.

You will need

- Pencil
- 3" (7.5 cm) heart-shaped cookie cutter
- Cardstock
- Scissors
- Glue stick
- Victorian print paper
- Diamond-shaped hole punch
- Computer and printer
- Moss green paper
- 1" (2.5 cm) circle punch, optional
- Round white tag with metal rim, 1½" (3.8 cm) in diameter
- Two large-hole beads
- Metal spacer bead

1 Trace the cookie cutter shape onto the cardstock and cut out the heart shape. Glue the heart to the back of the Victorian print paper. Cut the paper even with the cardstock heart. Repeat the process on the other side of the cardstock heart. Punch a hole in the upper right side of the paper-covered heart.

2 Create two 1" (2.5 cm) text circles on the computer in a word processing document. Type "sweet hearts" in one circle and the wedding couple's names and date in the other circle. Copy the circles as many times as will fit on the page. Print them on the moss green paper. Cut out the circles. Glue the names circle on one side of the tag and the "sweet hearts" circle on the other side.

3 Thread the beads onto the string of the tag. Push the paper heart inside the cookie cutter. Loop the knotted end of string through the punched hole in the paper heart. Tie the string around the cookie cutter. Bring the string of the tag around so that the tag lies inside the cookie cutter.

TIP **Use a star-shaped cookie cutter and a holiday greeting to make a favor for a Christmas cookie exchange party or holiday open house.**

Pearl–Wrapped CD Envelope

Create a CD containing your favorite love songs with legally copied music. Package the CD in an elegant folder wrapped in pearls.

You will need

- CD of songs
- Permanent fine-point marker
- Pocket-fold 5" × 5" (12.7 × 12.7 cm) decorative CD envelope
- 2 yd. (1.85 m) small pearl trim
- Two white wired leaves

1 Create the CD. Use the permanent fine-point marker to sign the CD with your names, along with a short message such as "with love." Insert the CD into the folder.

2 Wrap the pearl trim around the folder three times. Gather the pearl trim in the center front of the folder and twist together with one of the wired leaves. Twist the remaining leaf onto the gathered pearls. Curl any excess wire into a coil.

TIP **Instead of labeling the CD with the marker, use your computer and printer to create custom labels using self-adhesive CD labels available from office supply stores.**

Custom Blend Tea Package

Tea for two, and two for tea. This is a custom favor with lots of flavor.

You will need

- Heart patterns (page 109)
- Self-adhesive multicolor fabric
- Scissors
- 2¾" × 4½" (7 × 11.5 cm) mill cloth drawstring bag
- Orange flower appliqué
- Fabric glue
- Yellow cardstock
- Computer and printer
- White paper
- Glue stick
- Loose tea leaves of choice, 3 to 4 TBSP
- 2½" (6.5 cm) square glassine envelope
- Diamond-shaped hole punch
- ½ yd. (0.5 m) narrow orange satin ribbon
- Stainless steel heart-shaped tea infuser

1 Trace and cut out the heart patterns on page 109. Cut a large heart from the self-adhesive fabric. Remove the paper backing and adhere the heart to the lower right front of the mill cloth bag. Adhere the flower appliqué onto the heart shape, using fabric glue.

2 Cut another large heart from the fabric, remove the paper backing, and adhere the heart to the yellow cardstock. Cut the cardstock to the shape of the fabric heart.

3 Create a 1" (2.5 cm) square text box in a word processing document on the computer. Type "a custom blend" and the wedding couple's names and date in the box. Copy the box as many times as will fit on the page, leaving a margin around each box. Print the messages on the white paper. Cut out the messages. Glue a message to the yellow side of the cardstock heart, and trim the paper even with the edges of the heart.

4 Place the tea in the glassine envelope. Cut a small heart from the self-adhesive fabric. Peel off the backing and seal the envelope with the heart. Put the sealed envelope into the mill cloth bag and pull the drawstring closed.

5 Punch a hole into the upper right area of the cardstock heart. Slip the orange ribbon through the hole. Thread the ribbon through the handle of the tea infuser, and wrap the ribbon around the back of the mill cloth bag. Tie the ends of the ribbon into a bow in front, gathering all the elements together

TIP **To save time, you can scale back on the decoration of the mill cloth bag. Eliminate either the fabric heart or the flower appliqué. To achieve a very organic or natural style, you might also consider leaving the bag completely unadorned.**

Fore! Ever

This is a lighthearted favor for the wedding of a couple who loves to golf.

You will need

- Heart-shaped papier-mâché box
- 15" (38 cm) green/orange/gold
  plaid ribbon, 1½" (39 mm) wide
- Scissors
- Fabric glue
- Reindeer moss
- Golf ball
- Tiny orange and green heart stickers
- Computer and printer
- Off-white paper
- Sage green cardstock
- Orange coffee stir stick

1 Cut the plaid ribbon to fit around the heart-shaped box. Glue in place. Fill the box with moss.

2 Adhere the heart stickers to a blank area of the golf ball. Nestle the golf ball in the reindeer moss.

3 Create a 1" × 1¼" (2.5 × 3.2 cm) text box in a word processing document on the computer. Type "Fore! Ever" and the wedding couple's names in the box. Copy the box as many times as will fit on the page, leaving a margin around each box. Print the text on the off-white paper. Cut out the text, and glue it onto a piece of the remaining plaid ribbon. Trim the ribbon, leaving a narrow border around the text. Glue this piece to the sage green cardstock and trim, leaving a narrow border.

4 Glue the coffee stir stick to the back of the assembled tag. Cover the tag back with a piece of the plaid ribbon. Trim the stir stick to approximately 4" (10 cm) and insert it into the reindeer moss, behind the golf ball.

Message in a Bottle

Who can resist a mysterious message in a bottle? This favor is ideal for a tropical-themed wedding.

You will need

- Glass vial, 4" (10 cm) tall
- Small pieces of sea glass:
  blue, green, frosty white
- Small shells
- Green and white print paper
- Scissors
- 2" (5 cm) square green vellum tag
  with metal rim
- Computer and printer
- Light blue paper
- Medium blue watercolor pen
- Glue stick
- 12" (30.5 cm) turquoise yarn

1 Fill the vial approximately one quarter full with the sea glass and shells. Tear the green paper into a 4" × 5" (10 × 12.7 cm) shape. Write a short personal message on the plain side of the paper. Roll the paper up like a scroll and insert it into the glass vial.

2 Create a 1" (2.5 cm) square text box in a word processing document on the computer. Type the wedding couple's names and date in the box. Copy the box as many times as will fit on the page, leaving a margin around each box. Print the names on the blue paper. Outline each box with blue marker, rounding the corners. Cut out the names text and glue it onto the green vellum tag.

3 Tie the yarn around the scroll and onto the tag.

Modern Tussie-Mussie

Victorian ladies loved flowers, and the tussie-mussie, a small, cone-shaped paper filled with a dainty bouquet of posies, was a popular accessory. This fabric cone, a modern adaptation, can be filled with candy, flower petals, or any small treat.

You will need

- Square canvas coaster
- Fabric glue
- 6" (15 cm) spangled iridescent fringe
- Scissors
- "Romance" woven label tag
- 18" (46 cm) celery/black ribbon,
  ⅛" (3 mm) wide

1 Roll the canvas coaster into a cone and glue the end flap down. Glue the spangled fringe over the seam and trim any excess fringe. Glue the "romance" label along the upper edge of the cone, with the left edge overlapping the fringe heading.

2 Glue a length of the celery/black ribbon over the fringe heading, overlapping the left edge of the "romance" tag slightly. Trim off the excess ribbon.

3 Glue one end of the remaining ribbon to the inside of the cone, behind the lapped edge. Tie a knot near the other end, and glue it inside the cone on the opposite side, creating a handle. Fill the cone with the desired treat.

Love Sonnet Journal Cover

Few things in this world are more romantic than Shakespeare's 116th Sonnet. Here it becomes the cover of a keepsake journal or notebook.

You will need

- Ruler
- Scissors
- Cutting mat
- Silver pearlescent cardstock
- Aerosol adhesive
- 4" × 5½" (10 × 14 cm) spiral notebook
- Blue/pink/silver pearlescent paper
- Computer and printer
- Light blue speckled cardstock
- Dark pink pigment inkpad
- Silver cording with two tassels

Let me not to the marriage of true minds
Admit impediments. Love is not love
Which alters when it alteration finds,
Or bends with the remover to remove.
O no! it is an ever fixed mark
That looks on tempests and is never shaken;
It is the star to every wand'ring barque,
Whose worth's unknown although his height be taken.
Love's not Time's fool, though rosy lips and cheeks
Within his bending sickle's compass come;
Love alters not with his brief hours and weeks,
But bears it out even to the edge of doom.
If this be error and upon me proved,
I never writ, nor no man ever loved.

—SHAKESPEARE'S SONNET #116

1 Measure and cut the silver cardstock to 3½" × 5½" (9 × 14 cm). Spray the back of the paper liberally with aerosol adhesive and adhere it to the notebook cover. Tear the decorative paper to an approximate 3" × 6½" (7.8 × 16.3 cm) shape and adhere it to the silver cardstock, folding the excess top and bottom edges onto the inside front cover of the notebook.

2 Create a 2¾" × 4" (7 × 10 cm) text box in a word processing document on the computer, oriented in the portrait position. Type in the sonnet (below), followed by the wedding couple's names and the wedding date. Copy the text box seven times and place the boxes in two rows of four on the page. Print it on the light blue speckled cardstock. Tear the sonnet from the blue cardstock. (See page 10 for tips on tearing paper.) Lightly apply the dark pink ink directly from the pad all around the torn edges of paper. Allow it to dry. Using the spray adhesive, attach the printed sonnet at an angle to the notebook cover.

3 Lace the silver tassel cord randomly through the wire spiral of the notebook. Tie the ends in a knot at the bottom, allowing the tassels to dangle.

Glittering Basket

This silver filigree basket is a pretty favor to begin with, but weaving in some glistening metallic fibers adds a touch of magic. These colors and message were chosen for a Jewish wedding.

You will need

- 1 yd. (0.92 m) light blue metallic ribbon, ⅛" (3 mm) wide
- 1 yd. (0.92 m) white metallic ribbon, ⅛" (3 mm) wide
- 1 yd. (0.92 m) blue faceted metallic thread
- 1 yd. (0.92 m) metallic gold tapestry braid
- Plastic dental floss threader
- Silver filigree basket, about 2½" (6.5 cm) in diameter
- Silver and gold filigree shank button
- Scissors
- Ruler
- Pencil
- Royal blue cardstock
- Blue marbled paper
- Computer and printer
- White vellum
- ⅛" (3 mm) hole punch
- ½ yd. (0.5 m) light blue metallic braid

1 Thread the fibers onto the floss threader. Randomly weave the fibers in and out through the holes in the silver basket. Tie the fibers together on the outside of the basket. Use some of the fibers to tie the button in place. Trim the fiber tails to various lengths.

2 Cut 1½" × 1¾" (3.8 × 4.5 cm) rectangles of the royal blue cardstock. Cut slightly smaller rectangles of the blue marbled paper. Create a ¾" × 1" (2 × 2.5 cm) text box in a word processing document on the computer and add a wide rule around the box. Type "Mazel Tov!" in the box. Copy the box as many times as will fit on the page, leaving a small margin around each box. Print the text on the white vellum. Cut out the messages, leaving a narrow margin around each box.

3 Layer a blue cardstock rectangle, a marbled paper rectangle, and the vellum text, centering each inside the other. Punch a hole through all the layers of papers near the center top. Wrap the light blue metallic braid around the basket handle and thread the ends through the hole in the assembled tag. Tie the braid ends in a bow to secure the tag.

for
Women

Mini Shopping Tote

A tiny, plain favor bag gets dolled up with pink and black—just the thing for a modern girl. This favor can be used as a place card.

You will need

- White vinyl mini tote bag favor
- Pink/black polka-dot satin ribbon,
  ⅝" (15 mm) wide
- Fabric glue
- Scissors
- Black-and-white vinyl dot appliqué
- 8" (20.5 cm) pink 22-gauge craft wire
- Jewelry pliers
- Black rimmed round white tag
- Black permanent marker

1 Glue the polka-dot ribbon around the bottom of the mini tote. Trim the excess ribbon. Glue the appliqué onto the ribbon in the center bottom area of the tote.

2 Wrap the wire around the handles of the tote, creating spirals with the jewelry pliers. Write the guest's name on the round tag. Slip the tag onto the wire. Twist the wire to secure the tag.

TIP Little tote bags can be decorated to suit bridal showers, milestone birthdays, girls' night out parties, bridesmaids' luncheons, or bat mitzvahs.

Ribboned Bag

A small canvas tote can be elegant with some easy trimmings. Fill the bag with curled ribbons and tuck in some pastel candies, faux florals, bath oil beads, or tea lights.

You will need

- 8" × 6" (20.5 × 15 cm) mini canvas tote
- ½ yd. (0.5 m) Asian floral print ribbon, 2 ½" (65 mm) wide
- Fabric glue
- Scissors
- Two pearlized shank buttons
- Jewelry snips
- Tacky glue
- Stiff curling ribbon and treats

1 Glue the floral print ribbon around the top edge of the canvas tote, neatly trimming any excess ribbon.

2 Cut the shanks off the buttons with the jewelry snips. Glue the buttons onto the ribbon in the center front of the tote bag.

TIP **Canvas totes can be trimmed to suit any taste and occasion. Try a brown feather fringe trim and some wooden buttons for a fabulous natural look. A bright red boa trim with some rhinestone buttons makes a glamorously gaudy tote that would make Miss Kitty proud. Some black chenille rick-rack trim and a pink poodle appliqué will give the tote a fun retro look.**

Funky Fibers Trinket Box

Fill this colorful and fun keepsake box with the sweet treat of your choice. After the event, your guests can use them to store coins, earrings, or other small treasures.

You will need

- Oval satin fabric favor box
- Purple spray fabric paint
- 6" (15 cm) multicolored fringe
- Fabric glue
- Shaped wire flower

1 Spray the satin box randomly with the purple fabric paint. Allow it to dry.

2 Glue the fringe in a spiral onto the box top. Glue the wire flower on top of the fringe.

TIP **The contemporary style of this favor makes it ideal for bridal showers, bridesmaids' luncheons, a woman's milestone birthday, a bat mitzvah, a sweet sixteen party, or a quinceañera.**

Flower-Topped Box

This decorated box combines a natural look with rich colors. Inside, place a flower bulb, a bag of dried herbs, or a small packet of seeds.

You will need

- 3″ (7.5 cm) square papier-mâché box
- Copper leafing pen
- Dark green silk flower leaf
- Fabric glue
- Deep gold and maroon silk flowers
- Orange and green glass bead

1 Color the edges of the box top with the copper leafing pen, and allow it to dry.

2 Glue the leaf to the box top. Remove the blossoms from the flower stems and remove the flower centers. Glue the gold, then the maroon silk flower petals on top of the leaf. Glue the glass bead to the center of the top flower.

TIP **There are silk flowers to fit every season and mood. This favor could also be used for weddings, bridal showers, mother-daughter banquets, and special anniversaries.**

Treasured Friends Stickpin

Bits and pieces of pretty fripperies become a sweet piece of jewelry. For tips on cutting multiple ribbon strips, see page 10.

You will need

- Heart-shaped paper tag
- Lavender pigment inkpad
- Pink pigment inkpad
- Sage pigment inkpad
- Preprinted "treasure" sentiment
- Glue stick
- 10" (25.5 cm) pink satin fiber
- Micro hole punch
- Silver heart stickpin
- Liquid fray preventer
- 7" (18 mm) pink floral jacquard ribbon, ¾" (20 mm) wide
- 7" (18 cm) ochre twill ribbon, 1½" (39 mm) wide
- Scissors

1 Tap the lavender inkpad lightly and randomly onto the heart-shaped tag. Follow with the pink and the sage inkpads. Allow the tag to dry.

2 Tear out the word "treasure" and glue it onto the heart tag. Loop the pink satin fiber through the hole in the tag. Punch two holes into the heart tag approximately 1" (2.5 cm) apart from each other, above and below the word.

3 Place the pink floral ribbon on top of the ochre twill ribbon. Place the assembled heart tag on top of the ribbon layers. Attach the tag to the ribbon layers by inserting the stickpin in the top hole of the tag, through all the ribbon layers, and up through the bottom hole of the tag. Attach the end piece of the stickpin to secure.

Soy Candles on the Half Shell

Microwavable soy wax simplifies candle making. Make plenty of these pretty candles so you can use them to decorate your tables as well as to give them as favors. You can match the candles to your own color scheme by using a different dye. Please note: Follow directions and safety guidelines when working with hot wax. This is a project that requires your full attention. This is not a project for children.

You will need

- Tacky candle wax
- 2" (5 cm) pre-waxed candlewicks with metal disc clips
- Scallop shells, 2" to 3" (5 to 7.5 cm) wide
- Newspapers
- Microwavable soy wax (1 cup makes about 10 small candles)
- Microwave-safe liquid measuring cup, 2-cup capacity or larger
- Red liquid candle dye
- Microwave
- Oven mitt
- Wooden dowel
- Candle-making thermometer
- Scissors

1 Pinch off a small amount of the tacky candle wax and press it onto the bottom of the candlewick clip. Press the clip onto the center of the shell bowl. Repeat for each shell. Spread a thick layer of newspapers on your work surface. Lay the shells on the surface and prop them up to make the inner bowls of the shells as level as possible.

2 Place approximately 1 cup of the soy wax into the measuring cup, along with one drop of the red dye. Heat in the microwave 60 to 90 seconds. Use the oven mitt to remove the measuring cup. Stir the wax with the dowel to mix it with the dye. Continue microwaving and monitoring the wax every 30 to 60 seconds until the wax is melted and the temperature reads 180 degrees. Add more dye if a darker color is desired.

3 Carefully pour the melted wax into the prepared shells. Let the wax cool and set for several hours. Trim the wicks to about ¼" (6 mm).

TIP **These petite candles make wonderful favors for tropical theme parties, seaside weddings, or bridal showers.**

Bling Keeper

Bring on the bling! Give your guests a place to keep all their sparkly pretties.

You will need

- Glass votive candleholder with wide, flat rim
- Decorative bottle cap letters
- Metal glue
- Rhinestone heat-setting tool
- Eight heat-set crystal rhinestones, assorted colors

1 Wash the glass candleholder thoroughly and allow it to dry. Spell out the word "bling" with the bottle cap letters and glue them onto the rim of the candleholder.

2 Allow the heat-setting tool to warm up. Place the rhinestones between and to either side of the bottle cap letters. Set the rhinestones with the heat tool, following the manufacturer's directions.

Etched Mirror in Suede Pouch

A dainty mirror is slipped into a velvety-soft pouch. This favor is just the thing for a quick lipstick touch-up.

You will need

- 2" (5 cm) square mirror
- Glass cleaner and lint-free towel
- Glass etching flower stencil
- Masking tape
- Glass etching cream
- Paintbrush
- Red suede
- Scissors
- Leather cement
- Suede pouch template (page 110)
- Silver high heel charm

1 Clean the mirror thoroughly and allow it to dry. Position the flower stencil at the top center of the mirror and attach with the masking tape. Brush the glass etching cream over the stencil and let it work the amount of time recommended by the manufacturer. Rinse off the etching cream and dry the mirror.

2 Cut a square of the red suede to fit the back of the mirror and adhere it with the leather cement.

3 Cut the pouch from the red suede, using the template (page 110). Apply a thin line of leather cement along the edges indicated by the brackets. Fold the suede to create the pouch. Press the sides lightly to ensure an even adhesion.

4 Insert the mirror into the pouch and close the flap. Use a small dab of leather cement to glue the silver shoe charm to the front of the flap.

TIP **Though etching is a fun technique and gives the mirror a personal touch, omitting that step would save lots of time.**

Antiqued Mini Frame

Give a small frame an antiqued patina, then fill it with any image that fits the occasion. Many vintage images, like this seed packet, are available on a clip art CD. You can also use the frame as a place card. Just print out each guest's name in a lovely script font, and insert into the frames.

You will need

- 3" × 4" (7.5 × 10 cm) wooden picture frame
- Patina wax rub-on
- Soft cloth
- Image or photo to fill the frame
- Ruler
- Scissors

1 Remove the backing board and glass from the picture frame. Rub the surface of the frame randomly with the patina wax rub-on. Allow the wax to dry thoroughly. Buff the surface with a soft cloth.

2 Clean the glass and return it to the frame. Trim the image to the correct size and insert it into the frame. Replace the frame backing board.

TIP **If you are using clip art from a CD, size the image to fill the opening of the frame. Copy the image as many times as will fit on the page. Print it on ivory paper. Trim the image to fit into the frame.**

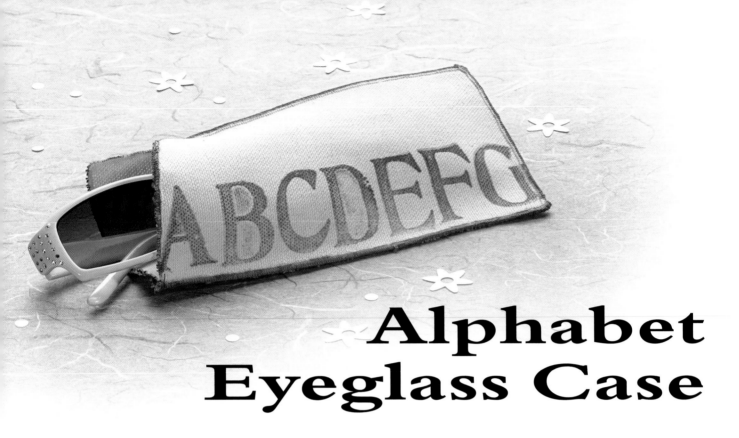

Alphabet Eyeglass Case

This is a fun favor that uses vintage alphabet stamps.

You will need

- Uppercase vintage alphabet rubber stamp set
- Ultramarine fabric ink
- Canvas eyeglass case
- Sienna fabric marker
- Ironing board and iron
- Press cloth or baking parchment paper

1 Apply ultramarine ink to the first row of the alphabet rubber stamp set (do not remove stamps from the acrylic backing). Press the row of stamps onto the left side of the eyeglass case.

2 Rub the ultramarine ink directly from the inkpad onto the back upper edge of the eyeglass case. Carefully run the tip of the sienna marker around the edges of the eyeglass case.

3 Set the iron to high, no steam. Cover the eyeglass case with a press cloth or parchment paper and iron approximately one minute to heat-set the ink.

TIP **This is a great favor for a special book club gathering or a school fund-raising event.**

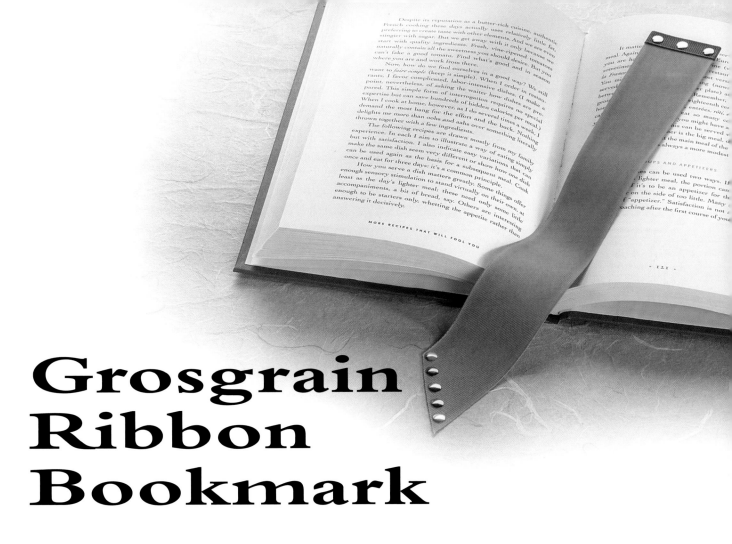

Grosgrain Ribbon Bookmark

Your guests can mark their place with this bright, jeweled bookmark. See page 10 for tips on cutting ribbons and preventing frayed edges.

You will need

- 12" (30.5 cm) lime green grosgrain ribbon, 1½" (39 mm) wide
- 5" (12.7 cm) royal blue grosgrain ribbon, ⅜" (9 mm) wide
- Scissors
- Liquid fray preventer
- Fabric glue
- Four gold metallic heat-set studs
- Two green metallic heat-set studs
- Two blue metallic heat-set studs
- Rhinestone heat-setting tool

1 Glue the blue ribbon across the top edge of the lime green ribbon, turning and gluing around onto the backside. Trim any excess blue ribbon.

2 Allow the heat-setting tool to warm up. Place the two green studs and one gold stud onto the blue ribbon band. Set the studs with the heat tool, following the manufacturer's directions.

3 Cut the bottom edge of the green ribbon on a diagonal. Use the heat tool to set the blue studs and the remaining gold studs along the diagonal edge.

TIP **Consider this favor for weddings, bar or bat mitzvahs, graduations, book clubs, or retirement parties. Choose ribbon and studs in the color theme of the event.**

Lavender
Bath Fizzy

drop into warm
running water
to dissolve

Bath Fizzy Bonbons

Spa-type items are always popular favors. One cup of bath fizzer base will make about six molded cakes. You can present the bonbons grouped on a cake plate or in a heart-shaped valentine candy box.

You will need

- 1 cup bath fizzer base
- Eyedropper
- Liquid cosmetic dyes: blue, green
- Lavender essential oil (or another scent)
- Mixing bowl
- Light bath and body oil
- Fork
- Water spray bottle
- Heart-shaped soap mold
- Tray
- Freezer
- Plastic wrap
- Pink flower sticker
- Computer and printer
- Pink cardstock
- Scissors
- Valentine print cupcake papers

TAG TEXT

Lavender Bath Fizzy
Drop into warm running water to dissolve.

1 Combine the bath fizzer base with two to four drops of the dyes and the scented oil. Add one teaspoon of the bath oil.

2 Spray the mold lightly with water. Press the bath fizzy mixture firmly into the mold. Let stand for 24 hours, and then carefully remove from the mold.

3 Place the bath fizzies on a tray in the freezer for several hours. Remove the fizzies from the freezer and carefully wrap them individually with the plastic wrap. Attach a pink flower sticker to the top of each wrapped fizzy.

4 Create a 1½" (3.8 cm) text circle in a word processing document on the computer. Type the tag text in the circle. Copy the circle as many times as will fit on the page, leaving a margin around each circle. Print the text on the pink cardstock. Cut out the text.

5 Place each wrapped bath fizzy in a cupcake paper. Tuck the tag into the cupcake paper behind the bath fizzy.

TIP To speed up the cutting process in step 4, invest in a 1½" (3.8 cm) circle punch. Turn the punch upside down and insert the paper, printed side up, so you can center the words in the hole of the punch.

Molded Glycerin Soap

Then deep blue color of this soap is reminiscent of soothing tropical waters. The delicate packaging is simple to create and will dress up a bathroom or vanity table.

You will need

- Glass measuring cup, 2 cup or larger
- ½ lb. (227 g) block clear glycerin soap (will make 10 to 12 soaps)
- Microwave
- Eyedropper
- Blue liquid cosmetic dye
- Essential oil in scent of your choice
- Wooden craft stick
- Flower-shaped soap molds
- Duo-sided paisley/pink heavy paper
- Ruler
- Scissors
- Pencil
- Round, shallow, metal tin with glass lid, 3" (7.5 cm) diameter
- Glue stick
- Decorative-edge scissors
- Small alphabet rubber stamp set
- Light blue dye inkpad
- ⅛" (3 mm) hole punch
- 6" (15 cm) pink yarn
- Plastic wrap

1 Put the clear soap into the glass measuring cup and melt it in the microwave on high power until liquefied, checking it every 30 seconds. Add a few drops of the blue dye and the essential oil. Mix thoroughly with the craft stick. Pour the mixture carefully into the soap molds. Let the soap harden on a flat surface for about 30 minutes. Remove the soaps from the molds.

2 Cut a 1¾" × 12" (4.5 × 30.5 cm) strip of pink/paisley paper. Remove the lid from the metal tin. Roll the paper, paisley side out, to fit the inside perimeter of the tin. Overlap the ends and glue them. Insert the paper ring into the tin.

3 Cut a 1½" (3.8 cm) square tag from the pink paper; trim one edge with decorative scissors. Fold over the decorative edge ½" (1.3 cm), forming a paisley flap. Stamp "relax!" with blue ink on the pink side of the tag, below the flap.

4 Punch a hole near the upper left side of the tag, under the flap. Loop the pink yarn through the hole. Tuck the ends of the yarn inside the paper-sided tin.

5 Wrap the soap in plastic wrap. Place the soap in the tin and replace the glass lid (the lid will now sit on top of the paper circle).

Custom Bath Salts

Encourage your guests to pamper themselves a little. Natural spa ingredients are packaged in a classy way.

You will need

- Dead Sea mineral bath salts
- Dried lavender buds
- Funnel
- 8" (20.5 cm) glass test tube with cork stopper
- Preprinted vintage cosmetic label
- Scissors
- Tacky glue
- Computer and printer
- Yellow paper
- Ivory scalloped tag
- ½ yd. (0.5 m) blue silk fiber

TAG TEXT

Bath Salts
Pour 2 to 3 tablespoons under warm running water
Ingredients: Dead Sea salt, dried lavender

1 Using the funnel, pour the bath salts and the lavender buds into the test tube, alternating the two ingredients in layers. Insert the cork into the test tube.

2 Cut out the vintage cosmetic label and glue it to the test tube.

3 Create a 1½" × 1" (3.8 × 2.5 cm) text box in a word processing document on the computer. Type in the tag text. Copy the box as many times as will fit on the page. Print it on the yellow paper. Cut out the text and glue it to the scalloped tag. Attach the tag to the top of the test tube with the blue silk fiber.

Keepsake Photo Album

An inexpensive photo album is easily transformed into a keepsake with a vintage look.

You will need

- Vintage clip art CD
- Computer and printer
- Off-white ink-jet printable canvas
- Ruler
- Pencil
- Scissors
- 4¾" × 6¼" (12 × 15.7 cm) photo album
- Fabric glue
- 1 yd. (0.92 m) blue lace trim
- 1 yd. (0.92 m) narrow bronze/gold trim

1 Print the desired image from the clip art CD onto the ink-jet printable canvas. Trim the canvas to fit the photo album cover and glue it to the album.

2 Glue the blue lace trim around the front and back edges of the album cover. Trim any excess lace. Glue the narrow bronze/gold trim on top of the blue lace trim

TIP The image shown was chosen for a bridal shower favor. Pick an image to suit your occasion. In addition to the album, hand out disposable cameras to your guests. They can shoot photos during the event, then put the prints into their albums.

Just
for
Fun

Japanese Basket

In Japan, the color red is associated with happiness. A red ribbon and the Japanese kanji character for "love" were added to this distinctive basket. Fill the basket with lotus flower potpourri, soothing incense cones, a favorite flower bulb, or a small scroll containing a lovely haiku poem.

You will need

- 15" (38 cm) red grosgrain ribbon, ⅝" (15 mm) wide
- Round basket with lid, 4" (10 cm) in diameter
- Scissors
- Fabric glue
- 22" (56 cm) black satin rattail cord
- "Love" kanji charm

1 Glue the red ribbon around the upper portion of the basket, trimming any excess ribbon. Apply small dots of glue near the upper edge of the red ribbon and adhere the black cord to the ribbon, leaving equal tails. Allow it to dry.

2 Tie the cord ends in the first step of a square knot. Slip the charm onto one tail, and complete the knot. Apply a small dot of glue to the knot to secure. Trim any excess cord.

TIP Present this favor at an Asian-themed wedding, a retirement party, a Japanese dinner party, or a graduation celebration.

Sun and Fun Rubber Ducky

This cute little duck will brighten up your bash and make guests smile.

You will need

- Small rubber duck
- 15" (38 cm) pastel stripe grosgrain ribbon, ⅛" (3 mm) wide
- 15" (38 cm) aqua picot satin ribbon, ³⁄₁₆" (6 mm) wide
- Tube of lip balm with sunscreen
- Silver sea theme charm
- Scissors

1 Tie the ribbons around the neck of the duck and then around the tube of lip balm. Knot securely.

2 Thread the charm onto one of the ribbon ends. Tie the ribbons in another knot to secure the charm. Trim the ribbon ends as desired.

TIP Consider this favor for beach weddings, pool parties, or baby showers. "Float" the ducks in a shallow bowl of clear marbles in the center of each guest table.

Plumed Pen

This posh plume will bring color, texture, and shimmer to your party tables.

You will need

- Neon green ballpoint pen
- 3" (7.5 cm) white feather trim
- Fabric glue
- Scissors
- 10" (25.5 cm) rainbow braided trim
- Glass taper candleholder

1 Glue the feather trim around the top of the pen and trim away any excess.

2 Glue the rainbow braid around the base of the feathers, trimming any excess braid.

3 Form a small ring of the rainbow trim and push it down into the base of the candle-holder. Insert the pen into the candleholder.

TIP **This favor can be used for bridal showers, graduations, educational fundraisers, bat mitzvahs, sweet sixteen or quinceañera parties.**

Movie Night Popcorn Box

Who doesn't like popcorn? This favor will be a blockbuster hit at your next celebration.

You will need

- Package of microwave popcorn
- Off-white textured paper
- Scissors
- Transparent tape
- One roll each red and blue ticket strips (sold in office supply stores)
- Glue stick
- Three adhesive pop-up dots
- Film canister sticker
- White tissue paper
- Vintage style popcorn box
- Black cardstock filmstrip die cut

1 Wrap the package of microwave popcorn in the textured paper, as if wrapping a gift. Secure the ends with tape. Wrap and tape one strip of the red tickets and one strip of the blue tickets around the package. Glue three tickets together in a fan shape; then cut into the ends of the fan, creating a fringe. Adhere this over the intersecting ticket strips on the wrapped package, using pop-up dots. Adhere the film canister sticker on top of the fringed tickets.

2 Build up the bottom of the popcorn box slightly with wadded-up tissue paper. Place the wrapped package into the popcorn box.

3 Thread a strip of the red tickets through the openings of the filmstrip die cut, allowing approximately 10" (25.5 cm) of tickets to hang from the top of the die cut. Push the filmstrip into the popcorn box, slightly behind the wrapped package. Curl the ticket strip around your fingers and let it fall over the edge of the popcorn box. Curl a strip of the blue tickets and tuck into the opposite side of the popcorn box, allowing the end to cascade over the edge.

TIP **This is an ideal favor for Oscar-watching parties, movie or Hollywood-themed parties, or fundraisers.**

Wine Stopper with Knob Top

Your local hardware store sells decorative drawer pulls in a wide range of beautiful designs. Bottle corks are available at craft stores, specialty wine shops, and through online wine-making Web sites.

You will need

- Wine cork, 1 ¼ " (3.2 cm) tall
- Crafting drill
- Decorative drawer pull
- Metal adhesive
- Purple print tag
- Tan vellum
- "Cheers" vellum sticker
- Gold paper brad
- 8" (20.5 cm) 22-gauge gold craft wire
- Flat-nose jewelry pliers

1 Drill a hole into the center top of the cork that will accommodate the stem of the drawer pull. Place a large dab of metal adhesive into the drilled hole and insert the drawer pull.

2 Adhere the sticker to the tan vellum and tear the vellum into a rectangle. Fasten the vellum to the tag with the paper brad.

3 Wrap the wire loosely around the neck of the wine stopper. Twist the wire around the brad and coil the end of the wire with the flat-nose pliers.

TIP **Drawer pulls are available in many shapes, sizes, and colors. You're sure to find a style that suits your occasion, whether it is a wine-tasting party, retirement party, garden club gathering, or bon voyage celebration.**

Wine–Tasting Journal

This is the perfect favor for a wine-tasting evening. Your guests can record their impressions of the wines sampled. You can adapt the project for other events, too; for example, use a silk flower head for a garden club event.

You will need

- Self-adhesive alphabet stickers
- Scissors
- Chianti pigment inkpad
- 3½" × 5" (9 × 12.7 cm) wooden notebook with window opening
- 1" (2.5 cm) craft cork
- Serrated kitchen knife
- Cutting board
- Tacky glue
- 2¼" × 2½" (6 × 6.5 cm) cork paper

1 Cut out the self-adhesive letters to spell "notes." Rub the edges of the letters lightly with the Chianti ink, directly from the inkpad. Allow them to dry. Remove the adhesive backing and adhere the letters to the front cover of the wooden notebook.

2 Carefully cut the craft cork in half lengthwise with the serrated knife. Take your time! The cork is fairly dense and it takes a little time to cut through it. Rub Chianti ink onto the lower half of the cork. Allow it to dry.

3 Glue the cork paper to the inside first page of the book. Glue the cork half onto the cork paper, making sure that the cork shows in the window opening.

Card Party Coaster

A tile can be turned into a coaster to suit the theme of your party. This one was for the guests at a bridge party.

You will need

- 4" (10 cm) square tumbled marble tile
- Mini deck of playing cards
- Tacky glue
- Playing card theme alphabet stickers
- Clear latex enamel spray gloss
- Cork paper
- Scissors

1 Glue a mini playing card to the tile. Spell out the word "play" with the stickers and adhere them along the bottom edge of the playing card.

2 Spray the tile with eight coats of the clear gloss, allowing each coat to dry thoroughly between sprayings.

3 Cut a 3¾" (9.5 cm) square of cork paper and adhere it to the back of the tile.

TIP **Make these coasters for other themed events. Clip art images of dice, dominoes, or bingo cards can easily be substituted for the playing card. Paper copies of old black-and-white photos would suit an "over-the-hill" birthday party. For a tropical-themed party, tear brightly colored tissue papers printed with parrots or palm trees and adhere to the tile.**

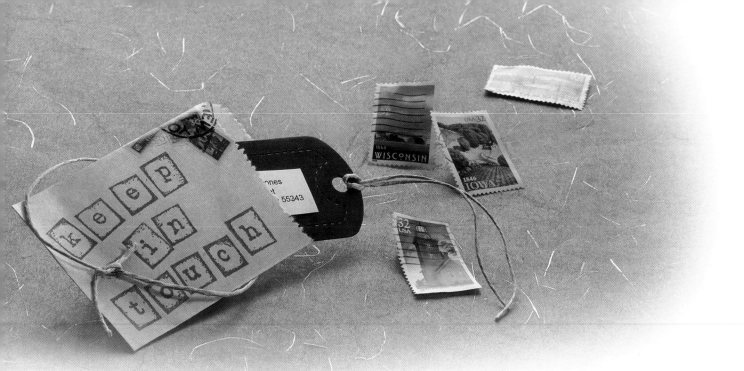

New Address Tag

This favor is a clever way to pass along a forwarding address at a moving-away party.

You will need

- 2½" × 4" (6.5 × 10 cm) mini brown paper bag
- Letter tiles rubber stamp alphabet
- Red dye inkpad
- Postage stamp stickers
- Cancellation mark rubber stamp
- Black dye inkpad
- ½ yd. (0.5 m) hemp twine
- Scissors
- Glue stick
- Black cardstock dog-tag die-cut shape
- Computer and printer
- Tan paper

1 Stamp "keep in touch" with the red ink onto the front of the paper bag. Adhere the postage stamp stickers to the top right area of the bag. Stamp the cancellation mark in black ink over some of the stickers. Allow the ink to dry.

2 Cut a length of the hemp twine to fit around the bottom area of the bag. Tie the hemp in a loose knot. Put a dot of glue behind the knot to hold the hemp in place.

3 Create a 1½" × ½" (3.8 × 1.3 cm) text box in a word processing document on the computer. Type the new address in the box. Copy the box as many times as will fit on the page, leaving a margin around each box. Print it on the tan paper. Cut out the message and glue it onto the die-cut dog tag. Loop the remaining hemp through the dog tag. Place the tag inside the paper bag.

BBQ Spice Rub Crate

This savory rub is a thoughtful and delicious favor. Feel free to change the color of the cardstocks or ribbons to coordinate the favor with your event.

You will need

- Spice rub ingredients
- Mixing bowl and spoon
- 3½" × 7" (9 × 18 cm) cellophane bag
- Transparent tape
- 12" (30.5 cm) orange/rust plaid ribbon, 1½" (39 mm) wide
- 12" (30.5 cm) narrow maroon ribbon
- Scissors
- Computer and printer
- Yellow cardstock
- Red cardstock
- Glue stick
- 5" × 3¼" × 2" (12.7 × 8.2 × 5 cm) wooden crate with handle

RECIPE

Ben's BBQ Dry-Rub Mix
I TBSP salt
I TBSP dry mustard
I TBSP paprika
½ tsp freshly ground black pepper
2 ½ tsp garlic powder

Mix ingredients together in a small bowl. Use a fork to break up any lumps. Pour into a cellophane bag and seal well with tape. Store in a cool, dry place. To use: Begin with a small amount of rub; you can always add more as needed. Firmly rub the mixture onto steaks, brisket, or pork chops. Shake off and discard any excess. Allow meat to sit for several hours in refrigerator, then cook or grill as desired.

1 Create the dry rub mix, using the recipe at right, and pour it into the cellophane bag. Roll up the bag and seal it with tape. Tie the ribbons around the bag and trim the ends.

2 Create a 3½" × 4" (9 × 10 cm) text box in a word processing document on the computer. Type the recipe card text (at left) into the box. Copy the box as many times as will fit on the page, leaving a margin around each box. Print it on the yellow cardstock. Cut out the recipe and glue it onto the red cardstock. Trim the red cardstock, leaving a narrow border around the recipe card.

3 Place the wrapped bag of BBQ rub and the recipe card in the wooden crate.

TIP **This favor would spice up any informal, outdoor, or Western-theme wedding, Father's Day BBQ, Fourth of July party, or fundraiser.**

BBQ Badge and Bandana

Form a posse of friends and make them honorary deputies of fun with these leather badges. The bandanas serve as napkins during the event.

You will need

- Precut leather sheriff badge star
- Metal alphabet punch set
- Mallet
- Brown permanent dye inkpad
- Soft clean rag
- Tie tack pin
- Quick grab permanent glue
- Bandana

1 Use the metal alphabet letters and mallet to punch "BBQ" into the leather badge.

2 Tap an edge of the rag into the brown inkpad and rub the ink randomly onto the leather badge, giving it an aged, weathered appearance. Allow the badge to dry thoroughly. Glue the tie tack pin onto the back of the badge, and allow the glue to dry.

3 Fold the bandana as shown. Pin the badge through several layers of fabric onto the bottom area of the bandana.

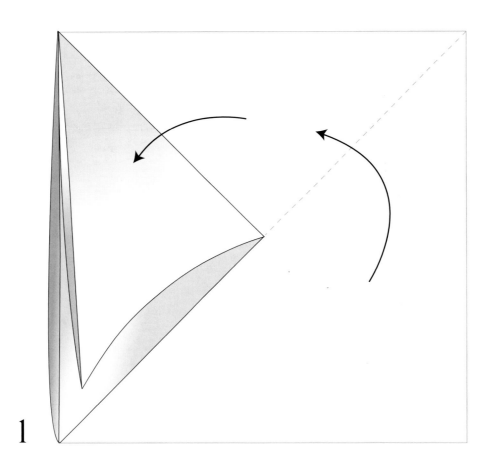

1

TIP Consider this favor for a BBQ
or Western-themed wedding.

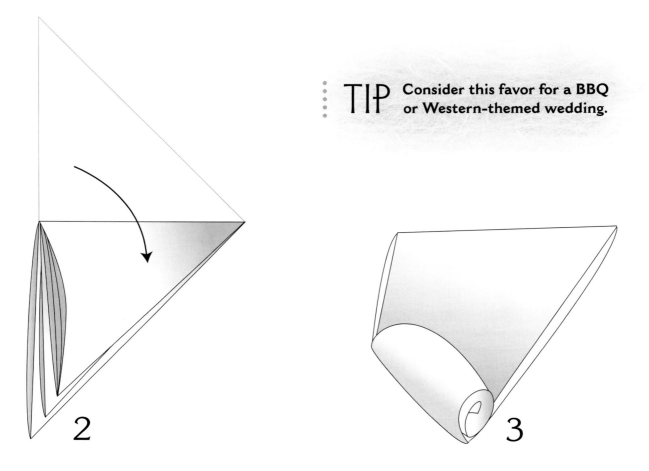

2

3

Stamped Chinese Door Hanger

The Chinese character for "joy" graces the front of this door hanger.

You will need

- 3" × 5" (7.5 × 12.7 cm) mat board
- Glue stick
- Lightweight red/gold printed paper
- Scissors
- Ruler
- Black corrugated paper
- Dark gold textured paper
- Red mulberry paper
- "Joy" character rubber stamp
- Black dye inkpad
- ⅛" (3 mm) hole punch
- 1 yd. (0.92 m) red cord
- 1 yd. (0.92 m) black cord

1 Cover one side of the mat board with a generous amount of glue. Lay the mat board, glue side down, onto the wrong side of the red and gold paper. Trim the paper, leaving a 1" (2.5 cm) margin around the mat board. To reduce bulk, trim each corner of the paper at a 45-degree angle, close to the corners of the mat board. Fold and glue the flaps of paper around to the back of the mat board. To give a neat finish to the back, cut a rectangle from the remaining red and gold paper and glue it to the back of the mat board.

2 Cut a 2⅛" × 4" (5.3 × 10 cm) rectangle of the black corrugated paper. Cut a 1¾" × 3¾" (4.5 × 9.5 cm) rectangle of the gold paper. Glue the gold paper onto the black paper.

3 Cut a 1½" × 2¾" (3.8 × 7 cm) rectangle of red mulberry paper. Stamp the "joy" character with the black ink onto the center of the paper and allow it to dry. Glue the stamped image onto the gold paper.

4 Punch a hole in the bottom center of the layered papers. Cut 8" (20.5 cm) lengths of the red and black cords, fold them in half, and loop them through the punched hole. Glue the assembled piece onto the center of the paper-covered mat board.

5 Cut a 3" × 1½" (7.5 × 3.8 cm) strip of the black corrugated paper. Create a casing at the top of the mat board by gluing the strip to the front and back of the mat board, leaving an open tube of paper at the top. Thread the remaining red and black cords through this casing and tie the cords in a knot approximately 6" (15 cm) above the door hanger.

Irish Charm Pin

Give your guests a bit of your love, friendship, and loyalty with this meaningful Irish pin. Claddagh is the name of the fishing village where this symbol originated.

You will need

- 4¼" × 5" (11.5 × 12.7 cm) dark green folded card
- Celtic knot rubber stamp
- Champagne metallic pigment inkpad
- Computer and printer
- Oatmeal-colored paper
- Craft glue
- ⅝" × ¾" (1.5 × 2 cm) silver frame pin
- Bronze metallic paper
- Scissors
- Silver Claddagh charm
- Toothpick
- Emerald green seed bead
- 12" (30.5 cm) green lattice-pattern ribbon, 1⅜" (35 mm) wide

CLADDAGH SYMBOL TEXT

The Claddagh Symbol
An Irish emblem of: Love (heart), Friendship (hands), Loyalty (crown)

1 Stamp the Celtic knot with the champagne ink randomly on the front of the green card. Set it aside to dry thoroughly. Create a 2" × 3" (5 × 7.5 cm) text box in a word processing document on the computer. Type the Claddagh symbol text in the box. Copy the box as many times as will fit on the page, leaving a margin around each box. Print it on the oatmeal paper. Tear out the text, leaving an approximate ½" (1.3 cm) margin to the left of the text. Glue onto the stamped green card.

2 Cut a piece of the bronze paper to fit in the recessed area of the silver frame pin. Glue the paper into the frame. Use a toothpick to dab small amounts of glue to the back of the Claddagh charm. Glue the charm on top of the bronze paper. Place a small dab of glue in the top center of the charm ring. Drop the green seed bead into the glue. Allow the assembled pin to dry thoroughly.

3 Fasten the pin to the green ribbon approximately 4" (10 cm) from one end of the ribbon. Place the pin near the top left area of the card. Wrap the ribbon around the card to the inside front. Lightly glue the ribbon to the inside front of the card. Leave the front ribbon loose so that guests may remove the pin and wear it.

TIP **Claddagh pins may be purchased online or from jewelry shops, thus eliminating step 2 altogether. This is an ideal favor for an Irish wedding or a St. Patrick's Day party.**

Glow Stick Necklace

When your party guests put on this festive glow-in-the-dark necklace, the fun begins. When it's time to glow, tell your guests the manufacturer's instructions for activating the party sticks.

You will need

- 5" (12.7 cm) glow-in-the-dark party stick
- 1 yd. (0.92 m) black cord
- Two silver jump rings
- Flat-nose jewelry pliers
- Three assorted charms
- Wire-wrapped green glass bead
- Large-hole green glass bead
- Large-hole fuchsia metallic bead
- Two scalloped white tags
- Computer and printer
- Purple paper
- Scissors
- Glue stick
- Silver brad

1 Fold the black cord in half and loop it through the opening of the party stick. Knot the cord securely next to the loop.

2 Thread a jump ring onto the black cord and slide it down next to the knot. Open up the second jump ring with the pliers. Thread the charms and the wire-wrapped bead onto the ring. Attach this to the jump ring on the cord, and close the jump ring.

3 Thread the large-hole green bead and the fuchsia bead onto the cord, and slide the beads down next to the jump ring. Knot the cord above the beads. Tie the loose ends of the cord together.

4 Create a 1" (2.5 cm) square text box in a word processing document on the computer. Type "Thanks for joining in the celebration!" in the box. Copy the box as many times as will fit on the page, leaving a margin around each box. Print the message in white letters onto the purple paper. Cut out the message and glue it onto one of the white tags. Place a tag on either side of the cord and fasten the tags to the cord with the silver brad.

TIP **This a fun favor for a party with dim lighting and dancing, or for a nighttime outdoor party. Teens and children will love it, too.**

for Life
Celebrations

Pink or Blue Coin Towers

These chocolate coin towers are quick to assemble and a sweet treat for baby shower guests.

You will need

- Three graduated size chocolate gold coins
- Glue stick or double-sided tape
- Flower rubber stamp
- Black dye-based inkpad
- Dark pink or blue cardstock
- ½" (1.3 cm) circle punch
- Light pink or blue patterned paper
- Ruler
- Scissors

1 Stack the three coins together. Secure them to each other with a bit of glue or tape.

2 Stamp the flower in black ink on the cardstock. Punch out the flower with the circle punch.

3 Cut the light paper into a 5" × ¼" (12.7 cm × 6 mm) strip. Lay the strip on top of the stacked coins. With glue stick, adhere the punched flower over the paper strip and onto the top coin. Bend and lightly crease the paper strip with your fingernail in a stair-step fashion down each side of the coin stack. Fold the strip around to the bottom of the coin stack. Adhere the strip ends together on the bottom, trimming to size.

TIP Coin towers can be used for lots of occasions. Simply choose papers in the color of your choice and pick a suitable rubber stamp.

Cherubic Dusting Powder

A standard powder container labeled with a sweet cherub paper will charm your baby shower guests. The container is filled with a custom-blended dusting powder. Try a combination of oils: lavender and patchouli are my favorites.

You will need

- 1 cup unscented baby powder
- Deep bowl
- 8 to 12 drops essential oils
- Eye dropper
- Fork
- Funnel
- White plastic baby powder container
- Clip art CD with cherub image
- Computer and printer
- Bright white paper
- Scissors
- Adhesive application system (or glue stick)
- Light green paper
- Decorative edge scissors
- Dark peach paper
- Tacky glue, optional
- Peach grosgrain ribbon, ⅝" (15 mm) wide
- Fabric glue

1 Pour the regular baby powder into a deep bowl. Add a few drops of essential oil at a time until you like the results. Mix thoroughly with a fork. Let the powder stand uncovered for about an hour. Break up any clumps that have formed. Use a funnel to transfer the powder to the plastic container.

2 Print a suitable image, like this cherub, from a clip art CD onto white paper. Trim the image from the paper. Use the adhesive application system (or glue stick) to adhere the image to the light green paper. Trim the green paper with the decorative edge scissors, creating a thin border around the cherub image.

3 Adhere the green paper to the dark peach paper, and trim the peach paper to create a narrow border. Adhere the assembled label onto the baby powder container using the tacky glue.

4 Glue the peach ribbon around the bottom edge of the label. Tie the ribbon into a knot at the center of the image.

Stenciled Baby Buggy Box

A raised design is easy to achieve using a stencil and heavy stencil cream. Fill the box with candies or a handful of potpourri.

You will need

- Heart-shaped papier-mâché box with lid inset
- Baby buggy stencil
- Low-tack artist tape
- Pastel stencil cream
- Palette knife
- White pigment inkpad
- Dimensional pink flower sticker
- Pink grosgrain ribbon, 1" (2.5 cm) wide
- Fabric glue
- Scissors

1 Remove the lid inset from the heart box. Tape the stencil over the center of the inset. Spread the stencil cream over the stencil with the palette knife. Carefully remove the stencil and wipe it off immediately. Allow the lid inset to dry completely.

2 Tap the white pigment ink directly from the pad onto the top of the box lid. Allow it to dry. Adhere the flower sticker to the bottom point of the heart box lid.

3 Glue the pink ribbon all around the heart box bottom. Trim any excess ribbon. Replace the stenciled inset into the box lid. Place the assembled lid onto the box.

TIP **Choose from a wide selection of available stencil designs to suit your particular occasion. A graduation cap, a flower, a wedding ring, a bell, or a star would turn this box into a completely different favor. Change the color of the stencil cream and the ribbon accordingly.**

Handkerchief Bundle of Joy

I used to pester my mother to make this imaginative baby bundle when I was little. I loved watching a lady's handkerchief magically turn into a baby snuggled in a blanket.

You will need

- Dainty white handkerchief
- Iron
- Blue and pink decorative fibers
- Rubber stamp alphabet set
- Blue dye inkpad
- Light blue paper
- Scissors
- Pink corsage pin

1 Press the handkerchief. Fold it in half diagonally. Roll the handkerchief along the fold from one point to the other.

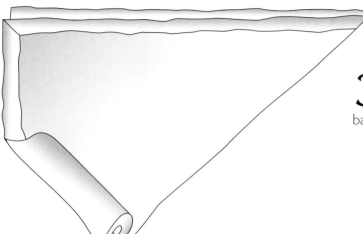

3 Turn the baby so the rolled edge is on top. Pull one side of the blanket up behind the baby. Pull the other side over the front.

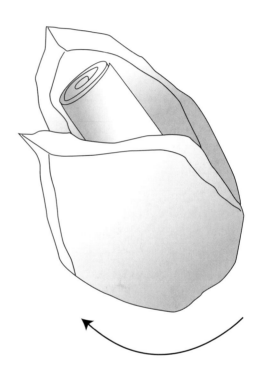

2 Holding the rolled fold (the baby) in one hand, pull the top two corners (the blanket) away from each other and downward until the points are even with the rolled edge.

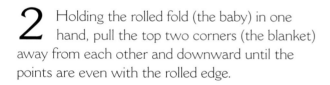

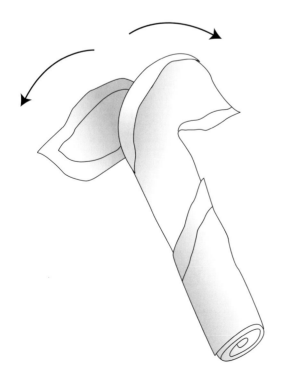

4 Tie the decorative fibers around the top portion of the baby shape, creating the suggestion of a head.

5 Stamp out "baby" (or the baby's name) in the blue ink on the light blue paper. Cut out a narrow strip of paper with the stamped word. Fold back the front of the blanket and pin the strip to the baby bundle.

Precious Baby Votive

You can customize this decorative votive candle favor to be predominantly pink or blue, depending on the sonogram!

You will need

- Straight-sided glass votive candleholder
- Pastel chenille trim, enough to fit around the candleholder
- Nonflammable tacky glue (check the label)
- Scissors
- Bottle cap embellishment
- Votive candle

1 Glue the pastel trim around the bottom third of the votive holder, joining the ends at the center of one side. Trim any excess.

2 Glue the bottle cap embellishment at the center front, over the joint in the trim.

3 Insert the candle.

TIP Bottle caps have made a comeback in a very unexpected arena—crafting! They are available at craft, rubber stamping, and scrapbook stores. They come in themed packages, such as wedding, holiday, baby, school days, and travel. They also come in packages of blank caps, ready for you to personalize with your custom-made messages or stickers. Most bottle caps come with self-adhesive dimensional foam on the inside of the cap. Simply peel off the backing and adhere the bottle cap to lightweight surfaces, such as paper or cardstock. When adhering to plastic, metal, or glass, use a tacky glue or a glass and metal glue.

Quinceañera Ribbon

A Quinceañera is a lovely Latin American tradition that commemorates a young girl's fifteenth birthday and marks her coming of age. It is a joyous celebration for family and friends and includes religious observances, special food, music, and dancing. In some countries, pretty ribbons are often fashioned into little pins and given as favors. The girl presents a pin to each guest as a way to say thank you for joining in her special day.

You will need

- 12" (30.5 cm) light blue silk moiré ribbon, ⅝" (15 mm) wide
- 12" (30.5 cm) narrow peach satin ribbon
- 12" (30.5 cm) narrow mauve satin ribbon
- Liquid fray preventer
- Fabric glue
- Antique white dimensional letter sticker (birthday girl's initial)
- Corsage pin with pearlized heart head
- Scissors

1 Lay the peach and mauve ribbons on top of the blue ribbon. Trim if necessary. Seal the ends with fray preventer. Lightly glue all the ribbons together in the center. Bend the layered ribbons into a graceful loop and glue the ribbons together where they intersect.

2 Glue the initial sticker onto the intersected ribbons. Insert the corsage pin through the layers of ribbon, behind the initial.

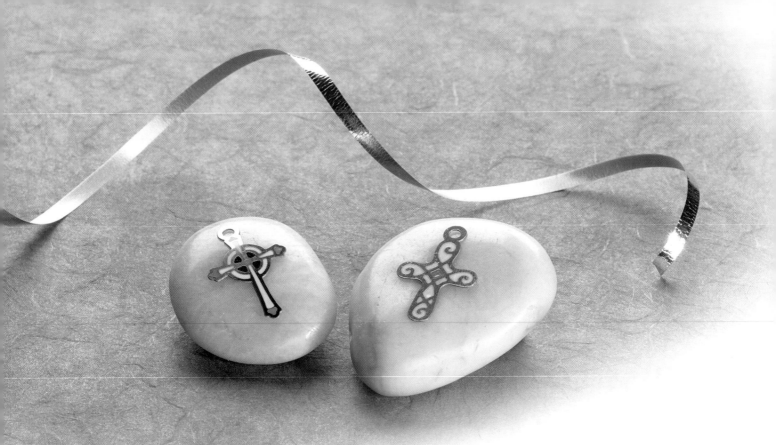

Decorative Cross River Rocks

This simple and beautiful combination of stone and metal is appropriate for an event held in celebration of a christening, first communion, or confirmation. The rock can be used as a paperweight or simply as an object to inspire quiet reflection.

You will need

- River rock
- Soap and water
- Soft cloth
- Decorative metal cross charm
- Metal glue

1 Clean the river rock thoroughly with soap and water and allow to dry.

2 Adhere the charm to the rock with a small amount of metal glue, gently bending the charm as needed to fit the contours of the rock.

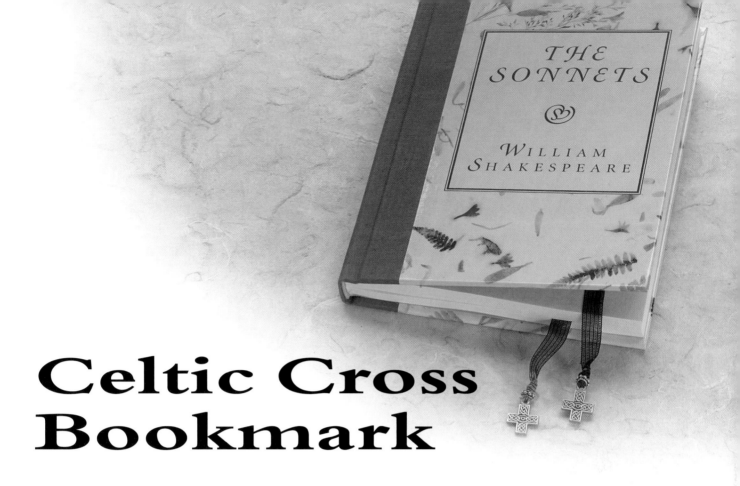

Celtic Cross Bookmark

The delicate interlaced lines of Celtic knot work remind us of our connections with all living things and the continuing cycle of life.

You will need

- 30" (76 cm) multicolor organza ribbon
- Two burnished silver Celtic cross charms
- Two silver spacer beads
- Scissors
- Fabric glue or liquid fray preventer

TIP **Present these bookmarks wrapped loosely around the napkins at place settings or inserted into programs.**

1 Thread a spacer bead onto one end of the ribbon and push it toward the center of the ribbon.

2 Thread a charm through the same end of the ribbon. Fold the ribbon end over about 2" (5 cm). Slide the spacer bead back toward the charm, over both layers of the ribbon. With the bead snug against the charm, knot the ribbon tightly just above the bead. Trim any excess ribbon close to the knot. To prevent fraying, touch the raw edge of the knotted ribbon lightly with a dab of fabric glue or liquid fray preventer.

3 Repeat steps 1 and 2 on the opposite end of the ribbon.

87

Graduation Party Pocket

Mark this special occasion with a cheery message of congratulations. Fill the pocket with a pencil, a glittery gel pen, a bookmark, or some stick candy.

You will need

- Jumbo manila shipping tag, 4" × 8" (10 × 20.5 cm)
- Bone folder
- Ruler
- Pencil
- Dye inkpads: sandalwood, sienna, red
- ⅛" (3 mm) hole punch
- Square plastic scrapbooking snaps
- Black permanent fine-point marker
- Word game mosaic tiles
- Tacky glue
- Computer and printer
- Tan paper
- Scissors
- Black cardstock
- Glue stick
- Black tassel cord

1 Lay the tag vertically on the work surface. Fold up the lower edge 2½" (6.5 cm) and crease the fold, using the bone folder. Tap the sandalwood inkpad randomly onto the flap. Repeat with the sienna and red inkpads. Allow to dry.

2 Punch holes through both layers on the upper right and left sides of the folded pocket flap. Insert the scrapbook snaps into the holes, and fasten them shut. Color the surface of the snaps with the black marker.

3 Gather the tile letters to spell out "Good job." Using the black marker, draw a smile face and a graduate's cap onto one of the Os. Arrange the letters as shown, and adhere them to the front of the tag pocket, using tacky glue.

4 Create a 2½" × 4½" (6.5 × 11.5 cm) text box in a word processing document on the computer. Type in the graduate's name and a message of your choice. Print it on the tan paper. Trim the message and glue it to the black cardstock. Trim the black cardstock to create a thin border around the message. Insert the assembled message into the pocket.

5 Loop the black tassel through the hole in the top of the tag.

Smartie Lightbulb

Celebrate an educational achievement with this smart little lightbulb.

You will need

- 2" × 5" (5 × 12.7 cm) heavyweight cream paper
- 10" (25.5 cm) each of three or four multicolored fibers
- 3" (7.5 cm) lightbulb-shape glass jar
- Smarties® candies

1 Hand-write or computer-print the graduate's name and date of the celebration on the paper strip. Roll the paper strip into a "diploma" scroll shape. Tie it securely with one of the fibers.

2 Tie the remaining fibers around the top of the lightbulb jar. Tie the diploma scroll to the fibers.

3 Open several rolls of the candies and pour them into the jar.

Silver Anniversary Photo Holder

Place these sleek photo holders on the tables at a milestone anniversary celebration. This favor also works well for birthday bashes.

You will need

- 1½" (3.8 cm) square wooden cube
- Silver and vellum heart stickers
- Craft knife
- Crafting drill with ⅟₁₆" bit
- 12" (30.5 cm) 18-gauge silver craft wire
- Flat-nose jewelry pliers
- Fat marker
- Metal adhesive
- Glue stick
- Wedding photo
- Silver metallic paper
- Decorative edge scissors
- Black cardstock
- Scissors

1 Adhere the heart stickers randomly around the wooden cube. Fold some of the sticker edges around the corners, and trim others off with the craft knife.

2 Drill a hole ½" (1.3 cm) deep into the center top of the wooden cube.

3 Bend the first inch of wire randomly with the flat-nose pliers. Wrap the next part of the wire two or three times around a fat marker to create coils. Pinch the coils together with your fingers, and then gently squeeze the coils even closer together with the pliers.

4 Put a dab of metal adhesive on the opposite end of the wire and insert it into the hole in the wooden cube.

5 Glue a wedding photo onto the silver paper. Trim around the silver paper with the decorative edge scissors. Glue the silver paper onto the black cardstock and trim the cardstock, leaving a narrow black border. Insert the photo into the wire coils.

Fabulous Fifty Golden Pushpins

Gold is the traditional color associated with fiftieth anniversaries. These easy-to-make pushpins are a unique way to add a touch of gold to the event.

You will need

- One package gold polymer clay
- Large ceramic tile
- Floral rubber stamp
- Baby powder, optional
- Oven
- Three clear plastic pushpins
- Quick grab permanent glue
- Foam-core board, ½" (1.3 cm) thick
- Craft knife
- Glue stick
- Floral swirl print vellum, violet/gold
- Scissors
- Invisible tape
- Scalloped manila tag
- Rubber stamp alphabet set
- Gold pigment inkpad
- Gold leafing pen
- 12" (30.5 cm) each of purple and gold metallic thread
- Ruler

1 Knead and soften the clay in your hands until it is warm and pliable. Roll the clay into three ½" (1.3 cm) balls. Place the balls on the ceramic tile.

Flatten the balls into discs, using the rubber stamp. (If the stamp sticks to the clay, sprinkle a tiny bit of baby powder on the stamp first.) Bake the clay on the tile according to the manufacturer's directions. When cool, glue the baked clay to the pushpins with the quick grab glue.

2 Cut a 1" × 6" (2.5 × 15 cm) strip of foam-core, using a craft knife. Cut the floral print vellum 3½" × 8" (9 × 20.5 cm). Cover one side of the foam core strip with glue from the glue stick. Center the strip, glue side down, on the wrong side of the vellum. Wrap the strip in the vellum paper as if wrapping a gift. Secure the back and edges with the invisible tape.

3 Stamp the word "fifty" in gold ink onto the manila tag. Stamp the small heart from the alphabet set just below the word. Allow the ink to dry. Run the tip of the gold leafing pen around the edges of the stamped tag, and allow it to dry.

4 Tie the metallic threads around the covered foam strip near one end, tying the tag into the bow on the front. Push the assembled pushpins into the foam strip, above the attached tag.

for
Holiday
Parties

Ring in the New Year

Make some noise at midnight with this glitzed-up bell.

You will need

- ½" (1.3 cm) circle punch
- Clock face clip art
- Scissors
- Glue stick
- Metal glue
- 3½" (9 cm) silver-plated handbell
- 18" (46 cm) each of five or six assorted decorative fibers
- Two to four small jingle bells
- Three to five spacer beads
- Decorative Mylar sheet, iridescent purple/green

1 Punch a ½" (1.3 cm) circle from the Mylar sheet. Cut the watch face from the clip art page. Use the glue stick to adhere the watch face to the Mylar circle. Use a dab of the metal glue to adhere the assembled piece to the handbell.

2 Gather all the decorative fibers together and tie in a tight knot around the neck of the handbell.

3 Thread the jingle bells and the spacer beads onto random fibers. Secure the bells and beads by knotting the fibers. Trim the dangling fibers to various lengths.

TIP **For an added touch, create a small tag with the new year printed on it, and attach the tag to one of the fibers.**

Key to My Heart

The flirty favor is ideal for a Valentine's party, though it can also be used for a wedding or anniversary celebration.

You will need

- 12" (30.5 cm) red decorative ribbon
- 12" (30.5 cm) multicolored decorative fiber
- Skeleton key
- Silver decorative tube bead
- Teal and orange marbled paper
- Round white tag with metal rim, 2" (5 cm) in diameter
- Scissors, optional
- Glue stick
- Computer and printer
- Off-white paper
- Fuchsia dye inkpad

1 Layer the decorative ribbon and fiber; fold in half. Insert the fold through the skeleton key opening and slip the tails through the loop to secure the ribbon and fiber to the key. Slide the tube bead onto the ribbon and fiber, so that it rests on top of the key. Knot the ribbon and fiber to secure the bead.

2 Cut or tear the marbled paper into an irregular square. Glue the paper onto the center of the white tag.

3 Create a 1½" (3.8 cm) square text box in a word processing document on the computer. Type "the key to my heart!" in the box. Copy the box as many times as will fit on the page, leaving a margin around each box. Print it on the off-white paper. Tear the message into an irregular shape. Tap the fuchsia inkpad around the torn edges of the message and allow it to dry. Glue the message onto the marbled paper.

4 Tie the tag onto one of the fibers or ribbons.

Spring Flowers to Go

C hinese food take-out boxes are fun containers; fill with fortune cookies, candies, or something unexpected, like a flower bulb. This favor was styled for a spring event or holiday. It would be perfect for a Chinese New Year celebration.

You will need

- Decorative purple take-out box
- 10 to 15 dimensional flower stickers, blues and greens
- Computer and printer
- Green paper
- Scissors
- Two white tag stickers with blue metal edge

1 Assemble the take-out box. Press the flower stickers randomly around the box.

2 Create a ½" × 3½" (1.3 × 9 cm) text box in a word processing document on the computer and type "Wishing you happiness & good fortune" in the box. Copy the box as many times as will fit on the page, leaving a margin around each box. Print it on the green paper and cut out.

3 Adhere the white tag stickers together, sandwiching the box handle and message between them. Add a flower sticker to each side of the white tag.

Patriotic Sparklers

This favor is for the Fourth of July or any patriotic celebration.

1 Gather the sparklers into a bundle and secure together with the rubber band.

2 Cut a 15" (38 cm) length of each ribbon. Tie the ribbons together with a knot at one end. Tape the knot to your work surface. Braid the ribbons together. Finish off with a knot at the end. Tie the braided ribbons around the bundle of sparklers.

3 Stamp "4th of July" onto the white tag. Tie the remaining ribbons together in a knot. Glue the ribbons to the white tag. Tie the tag to the bundle.

You will need

- Four sparklers
- Small rubber band
- 20" (51 cm) red narrow satin ribbon
- 20" (51 cm) white narrow satin ribbon
- 20" (51 cm) blue narrow satin ribbon
- Scissors
- Low-tack masking tape
- Round white tag with metal rim, 1½" (3.8 cm) in diameter
- Adjustable message rubber stamp (with choice of holiday messages)
- Red dye inkpad
- Fabric glue

Halloween Treat Bag

This grinning ghoul adds a spooky, silly touch to a little bag of Halloween treats.

You will need

- 4" × 12" (10 × 30.5 cm) brown paper bag
- Two dot patterns rubber stamps
- Black dye inkpad
- Orange dye inkpad
- Glow-in-the-dark rubber skeleton
- Glow-in-the-dark jack o' lantern pin
- Tacky glue
- 1 yd. (0.92 m) black cord
- 1 yd. (0.92 m) fuzzy rust yarn

TIP **The skeleton could be eliminated, and the bag would still look great with just the glow-in-the-dark jack o' lantern pin.**

1 Stamp the narrow dot pattern with the black ink three times along the bottom of the paper bag. Stamp the wider dot pattern with the orange ink twice along the bottom of the bag. Allow it to dry. Turn the bag over and stamp the narrow pattern in the orange ink along the top, pinked edge of the bag. Tap the black inkpad lightly along the pinked edges of the bag.

2 Glue the head of the skeleton to the back of the jack o' lantern pin; allow it to dry.

3 Fill the bag with desired treats and fold over the top of the bag. Fasten the bag closed with the assembled pin. Thread the black cord and the rust yarn through the opening in the fold and tie the fibers in a bow on the left hand side of the bag.

Thanksgiving Pyramid

A precut and scored pyramid box helps this autumnal favor come together very quickly. Fill the box with pumpkin seeds, candy corn, or chocolate coins, and put a box at each place setting.

You will need

- Assorted earth-toned cardstocks: maroon, eggplant, mustard, rust
- 1" (2.5 cm) circle punch
- Pyramid box
- Glue stick
- ¾" (2 cm) circle punch
- Three or four feathers
- 12" (30.5 cm) fuzzy rust yarn
- Ruler
- Pencil
- Scissors
- Computer and printer
- Ivory paper
- ⅛" (3 mm) hole punch

1 Punch four circles from the assorted cardstocks using the 1" (2.5 cm) punch. With the pyramid box lying flat, glue a circle to each side of the box. Punch five circles from the cardstocks using the ¾" (2 cm) punch. Glue four of the circles over the larger circles, varying the colors.

2 Glue two feathers over one area of punched circles. Glue another small circle over the base of the feathers to secure.

3 Fold up the box on the scored lines. Thread the yarn through the holes of the box top and pull the yarn to secure the box. Tie the yarn into a bow, leaving long tails.

4 Cut a 3½" × 1½" (9 × 3.8 cm) tag from the maroon cardstock. Create a 2¾" × 1" (7 × 2.5 cm) text box in a word processing document on the computer. Type "Happy Thanksgiving" in the box. Copy the box as many times as will fit on the page, leaving a margin around each box. Print it on the ivory paper. Tear out the text and glue it onto the maroon tag. Glue one or two feathers to the upper left corner of the tag. Punch a hole near the left edge of the tag, using the ⅛" (3 mm) punch. Tie the tag to the yarn tails.

Hanukkah Candle Set

This candle cup and decorated matchbox are for the Festival of Lights.

You will need

- Wooden candle cup, 1½" (3.8 cm) tall
- Blue pearlescent paint
- Paintbrush
- Silver leafing pen
- Two wooden dreidel cutouts
- Tacky glue
- Standard box of matches
- Blue/white print paper
- Pencil
- Ruler
- Scissors
- Glue stick
- 3½" (9 cm) royal blue grosgrain ribbon, ¾" (20 mm) wide
- 3½" (9 cm) silver grosgrain ribbon, ⅜" (9 mm) wide
- Fabric glue

TIP **This favor is meant to be symbolic. The wooden candle cup is not a safe holder for lit candles.**

1 Paint the entire candle cup with the blue paint. Allow it to dry. Color the rim with the silver leafing pen. Color the edges of the dreidel cutouts with the leafing pen. Allow them to dry. Glue one dreidel to the front of the candle cup.

2 Use the matchbox as a guide and cut the blue/white paper to cover three sides of the box (leave the striking side uncovered). Adhere the paper with the glue stick.

3 Adhere the royal blue ribbon lengthwise across the top of the box, using the fabric glue. Fold the ribbon ends to the inside of the box and glue. Repeat with the silver ribbon, gluing it over the center of the blue ribbon.

4 Color the edges of the dreidel cutout with the silver leafing pen. Allow it to dry. Use the fabric glue to adhere the second dreidel cutout to the box top.

Mitten Clip Place Card

Set one of these charming favors at each place setting of your holiday table. Afterward, guests can use the mitten clip as a tree ornament.

You will need

- Small green knitted mitten
- Eight small white pom-poms
- Fabric glue
- Mitten clip
- Snowflake rub-on decals
- Wooden craft stick
- Two round white tags, 2½" (6.5 cm) in diameter
- Glue stick
- Red/green striped paper
- Ruler
- Pencil
- Scissors
- Red cardstock
- White gel pen

1 Glue the white pom-poms across the wrist area of the mitten. Allow to dry.

2 Rub the snowflake decals onto the metal area of the mitten clip, using the wooden craft stick.

3 Glue the white tags together, using the glue stick. Cut the red/green striped paper into a 4" × 1⅛" (10 × 2.8 cm) strip. Glue the strip to the center of the tag. Cut a cardstock strip slightly narrower than the striped paper. Glue the cardstock strip centered over the striped paper. Trim the excess paper and cardstock even with the edges of the tag. Write the guest's name on the red cardstock, using the white gel pen.

4 Attach the assembled mitten and place card to the mitten clip.

Jingle Bell Bucket

Here is a jolly way to wish your guests a bright and shiny holiday season. Try mixing some red and green foil-wrapped candy kisses or tiny pinecones in with the jingle bells.

You will need

- Mini galvanized metal pail
- Decorative "Happy Holidays" bottle cap
- Metal glue
- Four holly motif polymer clay cane slices
- 6" (15 cm) holly motif ribbon
- Shredded paper
- 15 jingle bells, silver and gold
- Scissors

1 Glue the decorative bottle cap to the center front of the pail. Glue two holly cane slices to the right and left sides of the bottle cap.

2 Tie the holly ribbon to the pail handle. Fill the bottom of the pail with shredded paper and place the jingle bells on top.

Joy Candle Wrap

You can't go wrong with the classic holiday combination of red and green! Include a small gift card explaining that the wrap is merely decorative and should be removed before burning the candle.

You will need

- Red "joy" woven label tag
- ⅛" (3 mm) hole punch
- Four gold eyelets
- Eyelet-setting tool and hammer
- 18" (46 cm) narrow red metallic ribbon
- Scissors
- 2" (5 cm) diameter green votive candle

1 Punch a hole in each corner of the "joy" label. Insert an eyelet into one hole and turn the label around to the back side. Insert the setting tool into the small tubular side of the eyelet. Strike the setting tool with the hammer several times to set the eyelet. Repeat with remaining eyelets.

2 Cut the metallic ribbon in half. Thread one length through the eyelets on the top half of the "joy" label. Repeat with remaining ribbon on the bottom set of eyelets. Tie the ribbon ends together on the back of the candle and trim any excess.

Cafe Mocha Mix

1 1/2 cups instant coffee granules
1/4 cup unsweetened cocoa
1/4 cup powdered non-dairy creamer
6 TBSP confectioners sugar

Place all ingredients into a blender and mix
until finely ground. Place 1-2 tablespoons of the
mixture into a mug, add boiling water and stir.

Jar of Christmas Mocha

Pass out a tasty holiday favor that your guests can enjoy during the cold winter months.

You will need

- Ingredients for Mocha Mix
- Green decorative canning jar, 4" (10 cm) tall
- Computer and printer
- White cardstock
- Scissors
- Red die-cut mini envelope
- 20" (51 cm) red and white polka-dot grosgrain ribbon, ⅜" (9 mm) wide
- Silver "hope" washer charm
- Tacky glue
- Diamond-shaped hole punch
- Silver metallic narrow braid

MOCHA MIX TEXT

Cafe Mocha Mix

1 ½ cups instant coffee granules
¼ cup unsweetened cocoa
¼ cup powdered nondairy creamer
6 TBSP confectioner's sugar

Place all ingredients into a blender and mix until finely ground. Place 1 to 2 tablespoons of the mixture into a mug, add boiling water, and stir.

1 Create the mocha mix, using the recipe at left. Pour it into the canning jar, and close the jar lid.

2 Create a 3" × 2" (7.5 × 5 cm) text box in a word processing document on the computer. Type the Mocha Mix Text inside the box. Copy the box as many times as will fit on the page, leaving a margin around each box. Print it on the white cardstock. Cut out the recipe card. Place it in the red envelope and close the flaps.

3 Cut the red and white ribbon into two equal lengths. Slide the charm to the center of one ribbon, and glue it in place. Attach the charm to the bottom flap of the red envelope with a dot of glue. Wrap the ribbon around to the other side of the envelope and tie in a loose knot. Trim excess ribbon.

4 Punch a hole in the upper left corner of the envelope flap. Thread the remaining red and white ribbon and the silver metallic braid through the hole. Tie the envelope to the lid of the canning jar.

Frankincense Pouch

A regal pouch holds a fragrant offering of incense and your glad tidings of the season.

You will need

- 10" (25.5 cm) red/gold brocade wired ribbon, 4" (10 cm) wide
- Fabric glue
- 6" (15 cm) sage green satin ribbon, ⅜" (9 mm) wide
- Scissors
- 6" (15 cm) gold trim
- Computer and printer
- Off-white paper
- Gold leafing pen
- 2½" (6.5 cm) square glassine envelope
- Glue stick
- Frankincense and myrrh incense cones

1 Remove the wire from the brocade ribbon. Glue the sage green ribbon across one short end of the brocade ribbon, folding and gluing the edges to the inside.

2 Fold the brocade ribbon up 3" (7.5 cm) from the bottom, forming a pocket. Glue the pocket edges together.

3 Cut the free end of the ribbon at an angle. Glue the gold trim to the angled edge. Trim any excess gold trim and lightly touch the raw edges with fabric glue to keep them from fraying.

4 Create a 1½" × 2" (3.8 × 5 cm) text box in a word processing document on the computer. Type "Peace on Earth, Good Will to Men" in the box. Copy the box as many times as will fit on the page, leaving a margin around each box. Print it on the off-white paper. Tear out the text. Color the torn edges of the text lightly with the gold leafing pen and allow it to dry. Glue the text onto the front of the glassine envelope.

5 Fill the glassine envelope with four or five cones of frankincense and myrrh incense. Insert the envelope into the pouch.

PATTERNS

Text Panel (page 13)

Hearts (page 33)

Paper Cone
(page 13)

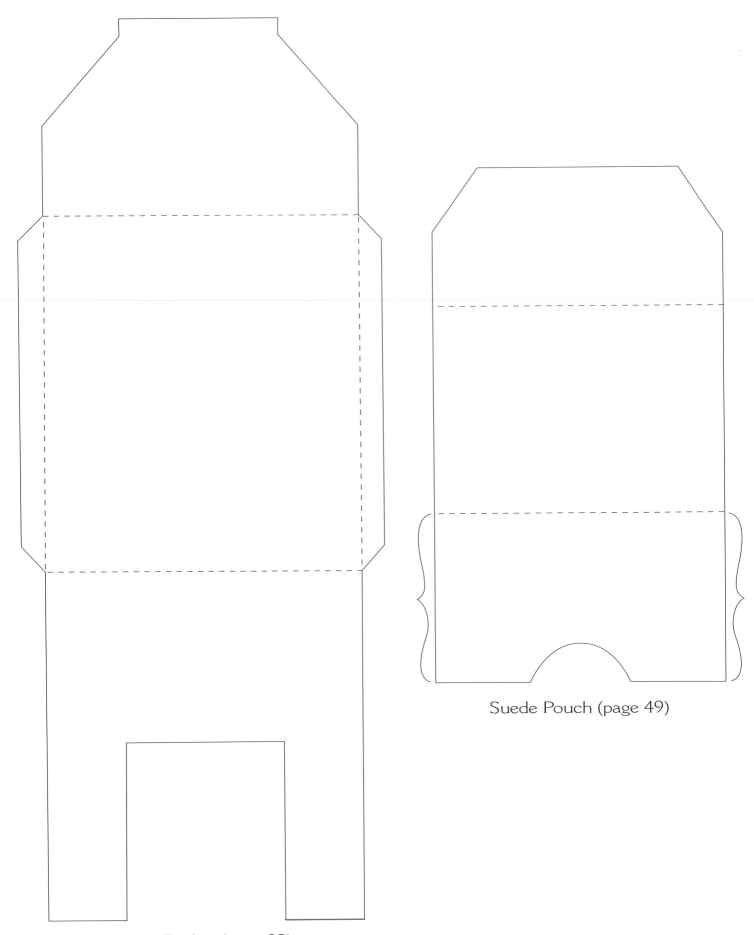

Paper Packet (page 29)

Suede Pouch (page 49)